新时代行业英语系列教材

总主编 姜 宏　　副主编 王卫华 陈英楠
主　编 黄 荣　　原版作者 Alison Smith

银行与金融英语
ENGLISH for Banking & Finance

清华大学出版社
北　京

北京市版权局著作权合同登记号　图字：01-2021-1541

© licensed by ELI s.r.l, Italy — ELI Publishing.
www.elionline.com
Author: Alison Smith

The English adaptation rights arranged through Rightol Media. （本书英文改编版版权经由锐拓传媒取得）

版权所有，侵权必究。举报：010-62782989，beiqinquan@tup.tsinghua.edu.cn。

图书在版编目（CIP）数据

银行与金融英语 / 姜宏总主编；黄荣主编. —北京：清华大学出版社，2021.4（2024.1重印）
新时代行业英语系列教材
ISBN 978-7-302-57793-5

Ⅰ.①银… Ⅱ.①姜… ②黄… Ⅲ.①银行业务–英语–高等职业教育–教材②金融–英语–高等职业教育–教材 Ⅳ.①F830.4②F83

中国版本图书馆 CIP 数据核字（2021）第 055443 号

策划编辑：刘细珍
责任编辑：刘　艳
封面设计：子　一
责任校对：王凤芝
责任印制：丛怀宇

出版发行：清华大学出版社
　　　　　网　　址：https://www.tup.com.cn, https://www.wqxuetang.com
　　　　　地　　址：北京清华大学学研大厦 A 座　邮　编：100084
　　　　　社 总 机：010-83470000　邮　购：010-62786544
　　　　　投稿与读者服务：010-62776969, c-service@tup.tsinghua.edu.cn
　　　　　质 量 反 馈：010-62772015, zhiliang@tup.tsinghua.edu.cn
印 装 者：北京博海升彩色印刷有限公司
经　　销：全国新华书店
开　　本：210mm×285mm　印　张：7　字　数：165 千字
版　　次：2021 年 4 月第 1 版　印　次：2024 年 1 月第 4 次印刷
定　　价：49.00 元

产品编号：091258-03

序

在经济全球化和国际交往日益频繁的今天，无论是作为个人还是组织的一员，参与国际交流与合作都需要具备良好的外语沟通能力和扎实的专业技术能力。高等学校承担着培养具有全球竞争力的高端技术人才的使命，需要探索如何有效地培养学生的行业外语能力。行业外语教学一直是学校的短板，缺少合适的教材是其中一个主要原因。目前，国内大多数学校在第一学年开设公共英语课程，所用教材多为通用英语教材，其主题与学生所学专业的关联度总体较低；部分院校自主开发的行业英语教材，在专业内容的系统性、语言表达的准确性等方面存在诸多不足；还有部分院校直接采用国外原版的大学本科或研究生教材，但这些教材学术性和专业性太强，对以就业为导向的学生来说，十分晦涩难懂。

清华大学出版社从欧洲引进原版素材并组织国内一线行业英语教师改编的这套"新时代行业英语系列教材"，以提升学生职业英语能力为目标，服务师生教与学。本套教材具有如下特点：

一、编写理念突出全球化和国际化

本套教材在欧洲原版引进优质资源的基础上改编而成，全球化视角选材，结合行业领域和单元主题，关注环境保护、人口老龄化、贫困等时代难题，培养学生的国际视野和世界公民素养。单元主题、板块编排和练习设计与国际接轨，体现国际规范和国际标准，且反映全球行业发展动态和前景，帮助学生全面了解全球行业现状和掌握国际操作流程，夯实行业知识体系。

二、编写目标注重培养学生使用英语完成工作任务的实际应用能力

为响应外语教学改革号召，培养具有国际竞争力的高端技术人才，将外语教学目标由原来的语言能力导向转变为职业能力导向，本套教材通过听、说、读、写、译等基本语言技能训练，让学生完成不同行业领域的工作任务，将英语放到职场的背景中来学，放到员工的岗位职责、工作流程中来学。

三、结构与内容紧扣行业领域的职场情境和核心业务

本套教材围绕行业核心概念和业务组织教学单元，不同单元相互关联，内容由浅入深、由易到难，循序渐进；教材各单元主题契合行业典型工作场景，内容反映职业岗位核心业务知识与流程。每本教材根据内容设置8至10个单元，用多种形式的语言训练任务提升学生对行业知识的理解与应用。

四、资源立体多样，方便师生教与学

本套教材图文并茂。通过改编，在原版教材基础上每个单元增加了学习目标，明确了学生在完成各单元学习后应该达到的知识和能力水平；增加了重点词汇中文注释和专业术语表，便于学生准确理解行业核心概念；听力练习和阅读篇章均配有音频，并借助二维码扫码听音的形式呈现，实现教材的立体化，方便学生学习；习题安排契合单元的主题内容，便于检测单元学习目标的实现程度。教材另配有电子课件和习题答案，方便教师备课与授课。教师可以征订教材后联系出版社索取。

本套教材共10本，包括《护理英语》《机电英语》《建筑工程英语》《运输与物流英语》《烹饪、餐饮与接待英语》《旅游英语》《银行与金融英语》《市场营销与广告英语》《商务英语》《商务会谈英语》，涵盖医药卫生、机电设备、土木建筑、交通运输、旅游、财经商贸等六大类专业。建议各学校结合本校人才培养目标，开设相应课程。

本套教材适合作为行业英语教材，也适合相关行业从业人员作为培训或自学教材。

姜宏

2021年3月31日

前言

在金融全球化、银行业务不断国际化的过程中，英语对于银行与金融从业者而言，变得尤为重要。本教材以提高学生的银行与金融行业英语能力为目标，在原版教材的基础上进行适当的本土化改编，以适应中国高等院校学生以及银行与金融从业者的学习需求。

本教材由银行系统、中央银行、商业银行、银行卡类型与诈骗、支付方式、证券交易所与商品交易所、财务数据解析、数字支付和申请工作等十个单元组成，带领学生了解银行与金融行业基础知识，培养学生的行业英语应用能力。每个单元均设有学习目标，让学生以目标为导向进行学习，主体部分由导入模块和听、说、读、写技能模块组成，课文部分均配有单词释义。

本教材既可作为高等院校银行与金融相关专业的行业英语教材，也可作为银行与金融领域从业人员的培训或自学教材。

本教材由黄荣、王卫华和陈英楠改编，黄荣负责第三至六单元和第九、十单元的编写，王卫华负责第一、二单元的编写，陈英楠负责第七、八单元的编写。为了使之更加符合中国国情，本教材还创新性地加入数字支付单元，邀请外籍教师James David Shipley和Lisa Diane Shipley夫妇参与编写。

本教材能够出版，首先要感谢清华大学出版社和总主编姜宏教授的信任，让我在英国伯明翰大学取得经济学硕士十年之后，有机会将所学应用到教材的改编中。编写过程中得到Shipley夫妇和北京财贸职业学院雅思教研室多位资深英语教师的帮助，总主编姜宏教授对本教材的审订，在此一并表示感谢。

限于编者水平，改编过程中不妥之处在所难免，恳请广大读者批评指正。

编者
2021年2月2日

Contents

Unit	Topic	Vocabulary	Skills
1 p. 2	Banking Systems	• Types of banks • Banking terminology	**Reading:** banking categories, microcredit, time banking **Speaking:** time banking **Writing:** microloan success stories
2 p. 12	Central Banks	• Common compound nouns for banking	**Reading:** UK, US and European Central Banks **Listening:** European Central Bank **Speaking and writing:** presenting a central bank and its roles
3 p. 22	Business Banking	• Types of accounts • E-banking terminology	**Reading:** business accounts and financing **Listening:** changes in UK High Street banking **Speaking:** advantages and disadvantages of e-banking **Writing:** the convenience of e-banking
4 p. 32	Types of Cards and Fraud	• Fraud and scams	**Reading:** types and use of different cards, understanding financial fraud **Speaking:** discussing different types of cards **Listening:** protecting yourself from fraud **Writing:** types of fraud carried out on the Internet
5 p. 42	Payment Methods (1)	• Terminology for payment and transactions	**Reading:** risks and benefits of international payment methods **Speaking:** discussing bank transfers **Writing:** analysing different payment methods

Unit	Topic	Vocabulary	Skills
6 p. 54	Payment Methods (2)	• Letters of credit	**Reading:** documentary collection and letters of credit **Listening:** opening a letter of credit **Writing:** an essay on documentary collection and letter of credit
7 p. 64	Stock Exchanges and Commodity Exchanges	• Market and trading terminology	**Reading:** stock and commodity exchanges, indices and brokers, key information on LSE and NYSE **Speaking:** working as a broker **Listening:** talking about stock market crashes and economic bubbles **Writing:** an essay on stock exchange
8 p. 76	Explaining Financial Data	• Changes and trends	**Reading and speaking:** understanding and describing charts and graphs **Writing:** a report on an investment portfolio
9 p. 84	Digital Payment	• Digital payment	**Reading:** two ways to pay via QR codes, two most common digital payment functions, China's digital payment trends **Speaking:** use of digital payments **Listening:** discussing digital wallets **Writing:** explaining advantages of Chinese digital payments
10 p. 94	Applying for a Job	• CVs and covering letters	**Reading:** how to write a CV and a covering letter **Writing:** preparing a CV and a covering letter **Speaking:** tips for a job interview

UNIT 1 Banking Systems

Learning Objectives

Upon completion of the unit, students will be able to:

- compare the main businesses offered by different types of banks;
- understand the contents of microcredit;
- understand how a time bank works.

Unit 1 Banking Systems

Starting Off

1 Do you know the names of any foreign banks? What countries are they from? Talk with a partner.

Reading 1

Types of Banks

Banking can be **defined** as the activity of accepting or **borrowing** money from **clients**, whether **individuals** or companies, and then **lending** out this money to other individuals or companies in order to **earn** a **profit**. Naturally the services offered by today's banks, as well as the types of banks in **existence**, are much more **multifaceted** than this.

Some **broad** groups of banking **categories** are as follows:

Retail Banks

These **deal** with individual customers and concentrate on mass market products such as current and savings accounts, **mortgages**, **loans** and credit and debit cards. All of the major retail banks in the UK also serve the needs of small businesses.

Commercial Banks

These deal with business clients, both large and small, and as well as current and deposit accounts, they offer foreign currency accounts and exchange, lines of credit and **guarantees** for international trade, payment processing, loans for business development and expansion.

Investment Banks
This kind of bank does not take **deposits** but works with companies and investment markets, for example by **underwriting** the issue of **stocks** or **bonds** and advising on **merger** and **acquisition** processes.

Private Banks
These manage the banking and financial needs of high net worth individuals.

Offshore Banks
These banks are located in countries which are considered tax **havens** due to low or no tax systems, and they offer financial and legal advantages to investors from other countries.

Building Societies
These are **mutual** financial institutions, which means that they are owned by their members. In the past their main business was savings accounts and mortgages, although now most have **diversified** and offer similar services to banks.

Postal Savings Banks
These are operated in **conjunction** with the national postal system of a country. When they were first introduced, they only offered savings accounts, however nowadays most of them offer complete banking services.

Unit 1 Banking Systems 5

MY GLOSSARY

define	v.	给……下定义; 说明, 解释
borrow	v.	借, 借入; （向……）借贷
client	n.	客户; 顾客, 主顾; 委托人
individual	n.	个人, 个体
	adj.	个体的, 个人的
lend	v.	借出, 借给; 贷款, 放贷
earn	v.	挣得, 赚得, 挣钱
profit	n.	利润, 收益; 好处
existence	n.	存在; 实有
multifaceted	adj.	多方面的, 多元的
broad	adj.	普遍的, 广泛的; 宽广的
category	n.	种类, 类别; 范畴
retail	n./v.	零售; 零卖
deal	v.	应对, 应付; 经营; 买卖
	n.	协议; 交易
mortgage	n.	（尤指购房的）按揭, 抵押贷款
	v.	（房屋）做抵押贷款
loan	n.	贷款, 借款
guarantee	n.	保证, 担保; 担保物, 抵押品
	v.	保修, 包换; 保证, 担保, 保障
deposit	n.	存款; 预付款, 定金
underwrite	v.	提供财力支持, 承担经济责任; 承保; 包销
stock	n.	股票; 储备物, 供应物, 存货
bond	n.	公债, 债券; 纽带, 联系
merger	n.	（公司、企业等的）合并
acquisition	n.	收购; 收购物; 购置品
offshore	adj.	境外的, 海外的; 近海的; 离岸的
haven	n.	保护区; 安全的地方; 和平之地
mutual	adj.	共同的, 共有的; 相互的
diversify	v.	多样化; 差异化
postal	adj.	邮政的; 邮件的
conjunction	n.	结合, 联合; 同时发生

2 Read the text and decide if the sentences are true (*T*) or false (*F*). If there is not enough information, choose "doesn't say" (*DS*).

		T	F	DS
1)	The principal aim of banking is to make a profit through borrowing and lending money.	☐	☐	☐
2)	Most private customers will have accounts with a retail bank.	☐	☐	☐
3)	Retail banks do not offer services to any kind of business.	☐	☐	☐
4)	Commercial banks are bigger organisations than retail banks.	☐	☐	☐
5)	A company interested in increasing its capital through new shares would consult an investment bank.	☐	☐	☐
6)	Private banks deal with people with a lot of money and investments.	☐	☐	☐
7)	Offshore banks are only located on islands.	☐	☐	☐
8)	Building societies and postal savings banks offer similar services to banks.	☐	☐	☐

Speaking 1

3 Work with your partner and discuss: What types of banks are mentioned in the text? What kinds of banks are there in China?

4 Have you ever heard of microcredit? What do you think it is? Talk together.

Reading 2

Microcredit

Microcredit is the concept of lending small amounts of money—microloans—to people who would not have access to such funds through **mainstream** routes. It was **conceived** in the developing world as a way to help poor people and **alleviate poverty**, and it is especially aimed at helping women and improving their position in society. Given that their aim is to help those at the bottom of the social **pyramid**, microloans are **granted** without the need for any **collateral**. Perhaps the most famous example is the Grameen Bank, which was founded by Nobel Peace Prize winner Muhammad Yunus in 1976 to provide credit to the poor people of his country, Bangladesh.

Since then, the concept of microcredit has become more widespread and is no longer **confined** to the developing world. For example, in the USA Grameen America is providing loans, training and support to those living on the poverty line so that they can build their own small businesses, improving the future for themselves and their families, while also **boosting** the local economy. Similar projects have been **launched** in the UK too.

In recent years there has been **criticism** of the microfinance system and its **claims** to reduce poverty and **empower** women in developing countries. Some experts argue that there is no evidence that microfinance projects have had positive impacts and, on the contrary, are in reality little different from **funds** from other financial sources such as moneylenders or banks. These **critics** believe that basic survival should come before growing a business, and microcredit ought to be combined with other **interventions** to improve financial **literacy** and understanding. If customers have no knowledge of how to save and plan for **repayments**, it is unclear how they are going to be able to **pay off** their **debt**. They therefore risk finding themselves in a worse position than previously when unable to pay off their loan. There may also be the **conflict** of whether it is possible for a bank or organisation to run a commercially **sustainable** operation while **simultaneously** maintaining its principles and values of caring about the **welfare** of those in need.

Microloan Success Stories

Name: Altagracia Damian
Country: Dominican Republic
Loan: $80
Business: Ceramics business

When she started her business, she had only 16 cents in her pocket. With her first loan, she purchased **clay** and **glazes**. Since then she has received a total of eight loans and now has seven employees and can pay for her children's education.

Microloan Success Stories

Name: Gonuguntla Mariamma
Country: India
Loan: $80
Business: Livestock farmer

Uneducated and **illiterate**, she bought a **buffalo** with her first loan to help provide for her family. With further loans, she managed to buy other livestock and now has four buffaloes, one calf and seventeen goats. She has also learnt to read and count a little and sign her name.

MY GLOSSARY

microcredit	n.	微型信贷
mainstream	adj.	主流的
conceive	v.	想象; 想出, 构想
alleviate	v.	减轻; 缓和, 缓解
poverty	n.	贫困, 贫穷
pyramid	n.	棱锥体; 金字塔
grant	v.	同意; 准予, 授予
collateral	n.	担保品, 抵押品
confine	v.	把……局限在; 限制
boost	v.	改善, 提高, 增强; 推动
launch	v.	启动, 推出; 发起
	n.	启动仪式, 发布会; 发射
criticism	n.	批评, 批判, 指责
claim	v.	声称, 宣称; 断言, 主张
empower	v.	授权; 使自主
fund	n.	基金; 专款; 资金
	v.	为……提供资金; 资助
critic	n.	批评者, 挑剔的人; 评论员
intervention	n.	干涉, 干扰
literacy	n.	知识, 能力; 识字, 读写能力
repayment	n.	偿还, 还款
pay off		偿还
debt	n.	借款, 欠款, 债务
conflict	n.	冲突, 分歧; 争论; 战斗
sustainable	adj.	可持续的, 能长期保持的
simultaneously	adv.	同时地
welfare	n.	福利; 幸福
ceramics	n.	制陶艺术, 陶器制造
clay	n.	黏土, 陶土
glaze	n.	釉, 釉料;（用来使食物有光泽的）浆, 汁
	v.	给……上釉; 给……上光; 使光滑, 使光亮
livestock	n.	牲畜; 家畜; 家禽
illiterate	adj.	文盲的, 不会读写的
	n.	文盲
buffalo	n.	水牛; 野牛

5 Read the text and answer the questions below.

1) What is microcredit?

___

2) Who are the normal recipients of microloans?

___

3) What is the Grameen Bank?

___

4) What is the purpose of microloan projects in countries like the USA and UK?

___

5) Why has there been some criticism of the microfinance system?

___

6) What is one suggestion to improve microcredit?

___

7) What risk can recipients of microloans face? Why?

___

8) Why could it be inconsistent for a bank to be both profit and welfare-led?

___

6 Match these words and expression with the correct definitions.

1) alleviate
2) poverty
3) collateral
4) empower
5) financial literacy
6) repayment

a ☐ to support and encourage
b ☐ valuable property
c ☐ the act of paying back someone or something
d ☐ to make a problem or situation less severe
e ☐ the condition of being extremely poor
f ☐ being able to understand basic principles of finance

Reading 3

Time Banking

The idea of using time as a means of exchange was conceived by Edgar Cahn in the late 1980s in the USA. Since then the concept of time banking has spread and there are now time banks all over the world. The idea behind time banking is quite simple: It uses time as a currency rather than dollars, pounds or euros. **Participants** "deposit" time in a time bank by offering a particular skill or service to other people, and then they are able to "**withdraw**" the **equivalent** amount of time and use it when they need some particular help or service. Time banking is based on the following **core** values:

- We are all valuable **assets** with something to give.
- The **definition** of work should include both economic and social activity, things like raising a family, building a safe **community**, caring for others and our planet.
- **Reciprocity** and how we can help each other.
- Networks of people are stronger than individuals and we need communities built on **commitment**, trust and support.
- Everybody is important. We must all recognise and respect the **contributions** everyone can make.

> Edgar Cahn, a former civil rights lawyer, started developing the idea of time banking after suffering a **massive** heart attack at age 44 which **radically** changed his **perception** of life. He is the author of several books, including *No More Throw Away People*.

MY GLOSSARY

participant	n.	参与者, 参加者
withdraw	v.	提取; 抽回, 取回; 撤回, 撤离, 退出
equivalent	adj.	等值的, 相等的, 等同的
	n.	等值, 相等, 等同
core	adj.	最重要的; 核心的
asset	n.	资产, 财产
definition	n.	定义, 释义, 解释
community	n.	社区, 群体; 社团, 团体

reciprocity	n.	互助; 互惠; 互换
commitment	n.	忠诚; 投入; 奉献; 承诺, 保证, 诺言
contribution	n.	贡献, 奉献; 捐款, 捐助
massive	adj.	严重的; 大量的
radically	adv.	根本上; 彻底地
perception	n.	看法; 知觉, 感觉; 洞察力

7 Read the text and answer the questions below.

1) Who developed the idea of time banking and when?

_____

2) What currency is used in a time bank?

_____

3) How does a time bank work?

_____

4) What fundamental principles are behind the concept of time banking?

_____

Speaking 2

8 **Discuss these questions in small groups.**

1) Do you think time banking is a good idea? Why / Why not?
2) How could it be helpful in times of financial crisis?
3) Will the concept of time banking increase in the future? Why / Why not?
4) Are there any time banks in China?
5) What skills and experience could you offer a time bank?
6) What help or services might you need from a time bank?

Writing

9 **Write a short essay (150–200 words) about microloan success stories in China.**

Technical Terms

current account	活期存款账户; 往来账户	deposit account	存款账户
		line of credit	信用额度
savings account	储蓄账户	tax haven	避税地
credit card	信用卡	building society	房屋互助协会
debit card	借记卡	postal savings bank	邮政储蓄银行

Unit 1 Banking Systems 11

UNIT 2 Central Banks

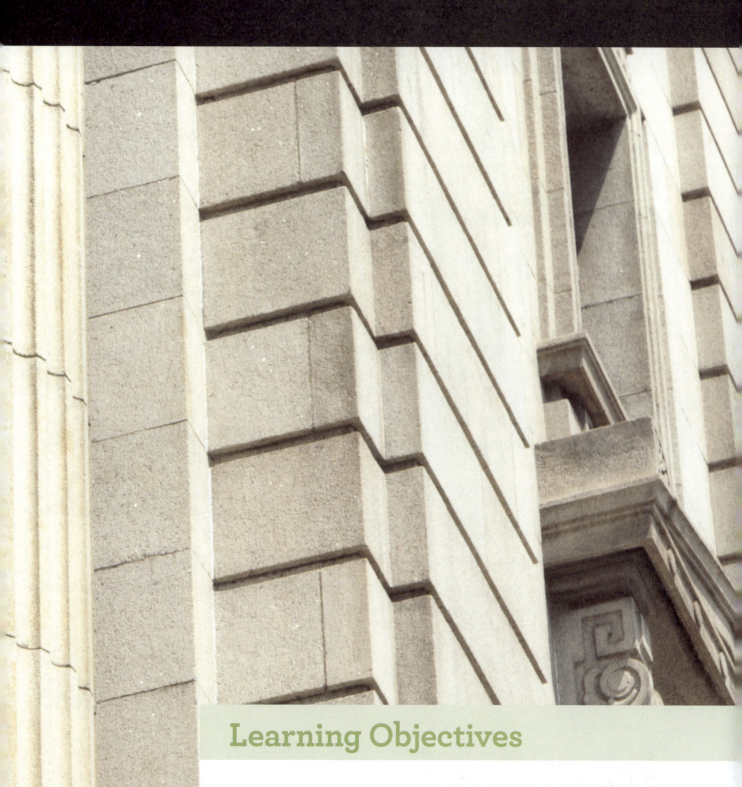

Learning Objectives

Upon completion of the unit, students will be able to:
- describe the functions and main objectives of a central bank;
- understand how a central bank can maintain price stability;
- compare central banks from the UK, USA and EU.

Starting Off

1 Is there a central bank in China? What is it called? What other central banks do you know? What are the core functions of these central banks? Talk together.

Reading 1

A central bank is responsible for its country's financial affairs and **monetary** system. Each central bank may have various specific tasks, **nevertheless** they can be said to have the same main objectives:

- to **oversee** monetary policy;
- to **maintain** price **stability** by controlling **inflation**;
- to manage the production and **distribution** of the nation's currency (issue of **banknotes** and **coins**);
- to support the nation in times of crisis to prevent its banking system from failing (providing funds to a country's economy when commercial banks cannot **cover** a **shortage**);
- to manage interest rates;
- to **serve as** a banker for other banks.

It is generally believed that a central bank can carry out these functions if it remains **independent** from, and **uninfluenced** by any political **regime**.

MY GLOSSARY

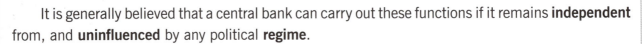

monetary	adj.	货币的, 金融的	coin	n.	硬币; 金属货币
nevertheless	adv.	不过, 仍然; 尽管如此	cover	v.	涵盖, 覆盖
oversee	v.	监督, 监察, 监管	shortage	n.	缺乏, 缺少, 短缺
maintain	v.	维持, 保持	serve as		担任, 充当
stability	n.	稳定; 稳固	independent	adj.	独立的, 不依赖的
inflation	n.	通货膨胀	uninfluenced	adj.	不受影响的
distribution	n.	分发, 散发; 分配	regime	n.	政权, 政体
banknote	n.	钞票, 纸币			

2 Read the text and answer the questions below.

1) What is the basic responsibility of a central bank?

_____

2) How can a central bank maintain price stability?

_____

3) How can a central bank support a country during a crisis?

_____

4) Should a central bank be guided by political parties? Why / Why not?

_____

Reading 2

The Bank of England

The central bank of the United Kingdom, known as the "Old Lady" of Threadneedle Street, was **founded** in 1694 to act as the bank for the government and to **handle** its debts. It has been independent since 1997, after 50 years of **nationalisation**. Today, its two core purposes are to maintain monetary stability and financial stability. In order to maintain price stability, the Bank's aim is to keep the **annual rate** of inflation at 2%—the target rate set by the government—and each month it sets the official Bank interest rate, independently of any government influence. The Bank is also responsible for maintaining financial stability, that is the public **trust** and **confidence** in the general financial system as well as the **institutions** and markets, which has become even more important since the financial crisis. The Bank's Prudential Regulation Authority (PRA) **regulates** individual financial firms, while its Financial Policy Committee (FPC) works to prevent or reduce any future financial crises. The Bank of England issues the nation's banknotes but not its coins, which are produced by The Royal Mint.

In the UK, there are banknotes in **denominations** of £5, £10, £20 and £50, each with the Queen featured on the front. In 2016, the Bank of England started issuing **polymer** banknotes instead of paper banknotes. This is thin, flexible plastic material which makes the notes cleaner, safer and stronger than the previous paper ones. So far they have issued £5 and £10 notes; the other two denominations will follow. All the banknotes have several different security features to make printing **counterfeit** notes as difficult as possible.

MY GLOSSARY

found	v.	创建，创立，创办
handle	v.	处理，对付，应对
nationalisation	n.	国有化
annual	adj.	一年一度的，每年的
rate	n.	比率，率
trust	n.	信任，信赖
confidence	n.	信心；信任
institution	n.	机构，团体；制度
regulate	v.	控制，管理，调节
denomination	n.	（尤指钱的）面值，面额；（某种宗教的）分支，派别
polymer	n.	聚合物，聚合体
counterfeit	adj.	伪造的，仿造的，假冒的

3 Read the text and decide if these sentences are true (*T*) or false (*F*). Correct the false ones.

                                                                                                               T   F

1) The Bank of England used to be a nationalised bank.   ☐ ☐

2) The Bank of England aims to keep inflation at more than 2%.   ☐ ☐

3) The UK government decides bank interest rates together with the Bank of England.   ☐ ☐

4) Maintaining public confidence in the financial system is part of the Bank of England's remit.   ☐ ☐

5) The Bank of England issues the country's banknotes and coins.   ☐ ☐

6) The UK has started using plastic banknotes.   ☐ ☐

Reading 3

The Federal Reserve System

The Federal Reserve System, also known as the Federal Reserve or simply "the Fed", is the central bank of the United States, founded by **Congress** in 1913. It **consists of** a central governmental agency—the Board of Governors—in Washington D.C. and twelve Regional Federal Reserve Banks located in major cities throughout the United States, each responsible for a specific **geographical** area and with one or two **branches**.

The Board of Governors' responsibilities include the **formulation** of monetary policy and the analysis of **domestic** and international financial and economic developments.

In addition, it **supervises** the operations of the Reserve Banks and has a **significant** role in the regulation of the US banking system.

Different US presidents and important figures are **depicted** on the banknotes: Washington $1, Jefferson $2, Lincoln $5, Hamilton $10, Jackson $20, Grant $50 and Franklin $100.

MY GLOSSARY

Congress	n.	（美国）国会；代表大会
consist of		由……组成，由……构成；包含
geographical	adj.	地理的，地理学的
branch	n.	分支；分公司
formulation	n.	制订，规划；构想；配方
domestic	adj.	本国的，国内的；家庭的
supervise	v.	监督；管理；指导
significant	adj.	重要的，有意义的
depict	v.	描绘，描述，描写

Unit 2   Central Banks

4 Read the text and answer the questions below.

1) What is the common nickname for the Federal Reserve System?

2) When was it founded and by whom?

3) Where is the Federal Reserve located?

4) How is the Board of Governors involved with the US banking system?

Reading 4

European Central Bank

Unlike other central banks, the European Central Bank (ECB), **established** in 1998 and **situated** in Frankfurt, is not responsible for the banking and financial matters of a single nation, but rather a group of nations. When the first eleven EU member states—and eight others at later **stages**—**adopted** the euro as their single currency, they no longer had monetary **sovereignty**. However each maintained its own central bank and together these now **comprise** the Eurosystem together with the ECB. The European System of Central Banks, on the other hand, includes the ECB and all the national central banks of EU member states whether or not they have adopted the euro.

According to EU **treaty**, the basic tasks of the Eurosystem are, among others:

- to maintain price stability;
- to **promote** the **smooth operation** of payment systems;
- to define and **implement** monetary policy;
- to manage foreign reserves of the Eurozone countries;
- to conduct foreign exchange operations.

The first euro banknotes were introduced in January 2002 and the second series, Europa, from May 2013. The €5 banknote started circulating in 2013, followed by the €10 note in 2014, the €20 note in 2015, the €50 note in 2017 and the €100 and €200 notes in 2019.

MY GLOSSARY

establish	v. 建立, 设立, 创立	comprise	v. 包含, 包括; 构成, 组成
situate	v. 使处于, 使坐落于	treaty	n. 条约; 协定
stage	n. 阶段; 发展时期	promote	v. 推进, 促进
adopt	v. 接受, 采用, 采纳; 收养, 领养	smooth operation	正常运转, 平稳运行
sovereignty	n. 主权, 统治权	implement	v. 实施, 贯彻

5 Read the text and match the information in the two columns.

1) 1998
2) Frankfurt
3) euro
4) Eurosystem
5) European System of Central Banks

a ☐ location of the European Central Bank
b ☐ the ECB and the central banks of EU member states using the single currency
c ☐ the ECB and all EU member states' central banks
d ☐ the single currency for some EU member states
e ☐ year the European Central Bank was founded

6 Match the words in the two columns to form compound nouns.

1) financial
2) interest
3) monetary
4) banking
5) single
6) foreign

a ☐ currency
b ☐ exchange
c ☐ crisis
d ☐ rate
e ☐ system
f ☐ policy

Unit 2   Central Banks   19

Listening

7 Listen to this presentation of the ECB and answer the questions below.

1) Who forms the Governing Council of the ECB?

2) Who owns ECB shares and how are they attributed?

3) What is the gold standard and when was it used?

4) With this method, why did central banks have to keep sufficient gold reserves?

5) What does the value of money derive from today?

6) Which of these roles of the ECB is not mentioned?

   A Defining monetary policy.

   B Issuing banknotes.

   C Keeping inflation low.

   D Managing foreign reserves.

8 Listen to the conversation and fill in the blanks.

A: Excuse me, Mr Sun. I'd like to know whether PBC (People's Bank of China) operates any banking business?

B: Being a central bank, the PBC doesn't operate any business directly, but it may use the (1) _____ to implement the (2) _____ .

A: I understand. What kind of monetary policy instruments may your bank use?

B: They include adjusting the (3) _____ and the minimum deposit reserve proportion, regulating rediscount and opening market operations.

A: Supervision and control of banking institutions and their business is a very complicated job, even in the (4) _____ . How do you take this?

B: According to the Central Bank Law, the PBC has the right to examine and approve the establishment, change and termination of the business scopes of banking institutions, because it has been empowered to audit, check and (5) _____ them.

Speaking

9 Do some further research on one of the central banks mentioned in this unit and prepare a short presentation (3–5 minutes). Include these points:

- its foundation and organisational structure;
- its main roles and responsibilities;
- any criticisms of its operations, for example, during the latest financial crisis.

Writing

10 Write a short essay (150–200 words) to explain the general roles of the central bank in China and its objectives.

Technical Terms

interest rate 利率
Threadneedle Street 针线街（英国伦敦的金融街）
Prudential Regulation Authority 英国审慎监管局
Financial Policy Committee 金融政策委员会
The Royal Mint 英国皇家造币厂

The Federal Reserve System 联邦储备体系
the Board of Governors 联邦储备委员会
European System of Central Banks 欧洲中央银行体系
foreign reserves 外汇储备
foreign exchange 外汇

Unit 2 Central Banks 21

UNIT 3 Business Banking

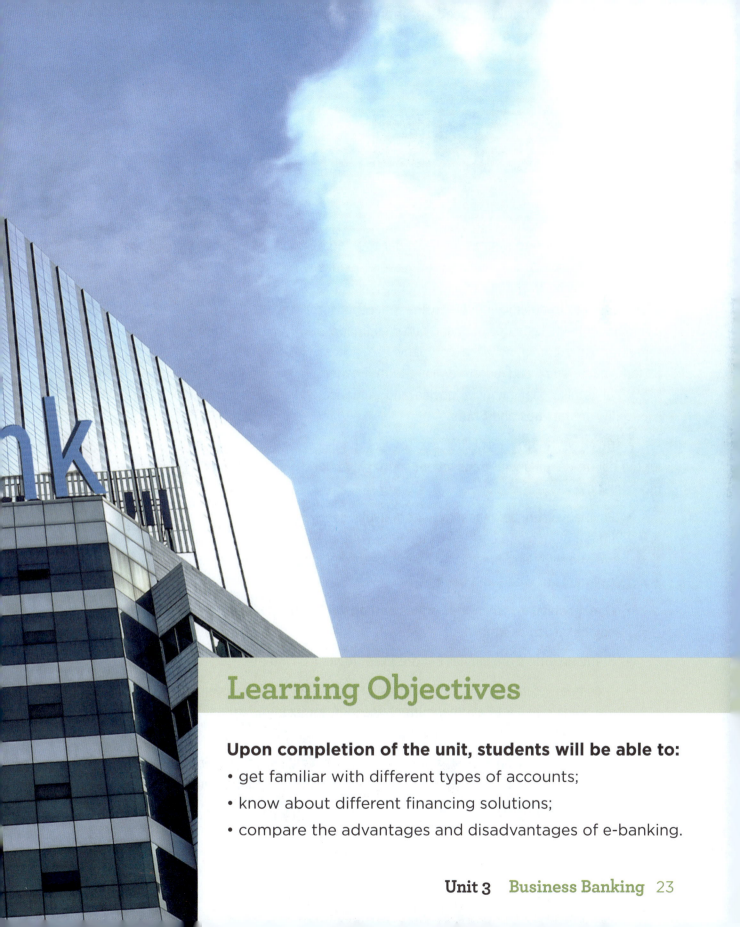

Learning Objectives

Upon completion of the unit, students will be able to:
- get familiar with different types of accounts;
- know about different financing solutions;
- compare the advantages and disadvantages of e-banking.

Unit 3   Business Banking

Starting Off

1 Do you think the banking needs of individuals and businesses are the same? Why / Why not? Discuss with your partner.

Reading 1

Types of Accounts

Any kind of business, from a sole trader to a large **multinational**, needs a bank or even several banks and their services to handle their financial needs and enable them to trade efficiently. A business account for a sole trader helps keep business and personal finances separate, for example, while a company has access to foreign currency and short- or long-term finance. Many banks also offer financial advice and guidance, especially for **start-ups** and **SMEs**.

Current Account This is used by companies for the day-to-day financial **transactions** of making and receiving payments.

- Payments can be made by withdrawing cash from a branch or a cash machine or by writing a **cheque**, although these have mainly been replaced by more efficient and quicker automatic payments or credit and debit cards.

- Direct debits are when the bank is **authorised** to take payment directly from the account to pay bills such as utility bills.

- Standing orders are similar but are fixed, regular payments.

- A company can also give **instructions** for a credit or bank transfer which is when payments are made directly to another current account, for example, to pay a supplier. The company can also receive payments in this way.

There are normally bank **charges** for all these transactions. To **keep track of** these movements, banks supply regular account statements, which can also be **consulted** online.

Deposit Account A deposit or savings account usually pays interest and it may be necessary to give advance warning before withdrawing funds. Nowadays, they are not so widely used as companies may have few surplus funds to deposit or they will invest in other financial products and investment schemes.

Foreign Currency Account Clients who trade internationally can have accounts with their bank in different currencies, which can resolve problems connected with **fluctuations** in exchange rates.

MY GLOSSARY

multinational	n.	跨国公司
start-up	n.	初创企业
SME	abbr.	中小企业（small and medium-sized enterprise）
transaction	n.	交易
cheque	n.	支票
authorise	v.	授权，批准，允许

instruction	n.	指令，指示；说明
charge	n.	费用；掌管
keep track of		记录，追踪；与……保持联系
consult	v.	查阅；商量；咨询
fluctuation	n.	波动

2 Read the text and answer the questions below.

1) What is the difference between a current account and a deposit account?

_____

2) Why are cash and cheques no longer so popular?

_____

3) What is the advantage of standing orders and direct debits for an account holder?

_____

4) When are bank transfers used?

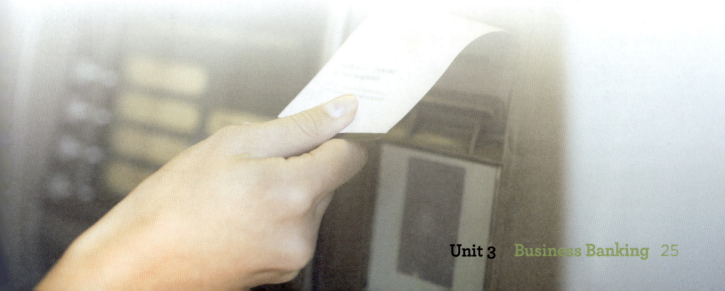

Unit 3 Business Banking 25

Reading 2

Financing

Overdraft This is an agreement where the client is allowed to spend more money than is actually in the account, often called "going into the red". As **overdrafts are** normally **subject to** high interest rates and heavy bank charges, they are really only a short-term **solution** to cover emergency situations and **temporary** lack of funds.

Loans Unlike overdrafts, loans are a more suitable means for short- and medium-term financing. They can be granted, for example, to expand a business or to cover a period of difficulty. Commercial mortgages are a way of obtaining long-term **capital**, for example to buy a **property** or another business.

Leasing This is a method of purchasing equipment, **machinery** or other assets without having to pay the full amount upfront. The company pays a **fee** to the bank or finance company for a fixed period of time which allows the use of the equipment. Additional advantages are that these payments are often **tax-deductible** and the agreement can include the free **maintenance** or **replacement** with **updated** models. Leasing opportunities are now also offered directly by companies such as car manufacturers and office equipment suppliers.

MY GLOSSARY

overdraft	n.	透支; 透支额
be subject to		有……倾向的; 受……支配
solution	n.	解决方案
temporary	adj.	暂时的, 临时的
capital	n.	资本, 资金; 本钱
property	n.	房地产; 性质, 性能; 财产
leasing	n.	租赁
machinery	n.	机械, 机器
fee	n.	费用
tax-deductible	adj.	可免税的
maintenance	n.	维护, 维修
replacement	n.	更换, 替换
updated	adj.	更新的; 现代化的

3 Read the text and answer the questions below.

1) Why are overdrafts only a short-term financing solution?

2) What financing solutions can banks offer in the medium and long term?

3) Why does a company need finance from a bank?

4) What advantages does a leasing agreement have for a company?

5) What kind of goods are leasing agreements usually for?

Reading 3

E-Banking

Internet Banking It allows private customers and businesses to manage their bank accounts and carry out traditional banking operations like checking bank statements, paying **bills** and transferring funds online. It is also possible to have access to other services such as loan applications, financial products and stock market investments. Internet banking services are provided by both **"bricks and mortar"** banks and online banks. The former is a bank with physical branches that also offers Internet banking, the latter operates **exclusively** online.

Mobile Banking It is when a bank account, credit card or other financial account can be accessed using a smartphone or similar device. This can be via Internet access to a bank's home page, text messaging or by using one of the many apps from banks for handling various financial transactions.

Mobile payment, often called mobile wallet, is the process in which mobile phones are loaded and stored with money which is then used to make payments.

Both these services are increasing in popularity in the Western world, but even more so in those parts of the world where physical banks are more difficult to reach due to long distances and also, in the case of mobile wallets, for the unbanked, those people who do not have access to any kind of bank account.

Advantages

- 24/7 availability: You can access your account and related services whenever and wherever you want.

- No wasted time: There is no need to waste time going into a branch and waiting in a long queue.

- Real time: You can immediately access updated financial statements and check your account balance.

- Cost-effective: Account costs are usually less than for a traditional account.

- Environmentally-friendly: There is no need for the bank or the client to print and send documents and statements as it is all stored electronically.

Disadvantages

- Security issues: Most online banking operations are secure thanks to **encryption** techniques but there still may be a risk.

- Identity theft: There is a risk of your identity and bank details being stolen and used **fraudulently**.

- Lack of contact: For some people, the lack of personal contact can be a problem and they prefer being able to speak to someone directly about their account matters.

- **Dependability**: In the case of online banks, it is advisable to check their reliability and background, as well as their **registration** with national **regulatory** bodies.

- Computer **illiteracy**: Online accounts are not suitable for those who are not good or confident at using computers nor, obviously, for those with no Internet access.

MY GLOSSARY

bill	n.	账单		fraudulently	adv.	欺骗地
bricks and mortar		实体的（由砖头水泥建造而成的）		dependability	n.	可靠性；可信任
				registration	n.	登记，注册
exclusively	adv.	专有地，排外地		regulatory	adj.	管理的，控制的
encryption	n.	加密；加密术		illiteracy	n.	文盲

4 Read the text and match the two halves of the sentences.

1) Internet banking is aimed
2) Traditional accounts may have
3) Not having to print documents means
4) Online banks registered with the regulatory authorities
5) By downloading a bank app you can
6) Mobile payment has many benefits

a ☐ for people in remote areas.
b ☐ carry out financial transactions on your mobile phone.
c ☐ are safe for clients to use.
d ☐ at both private and business customers.
e ☐ online banks are environmentally-friendly.
f ☐ more bank charges than online ones.

5 Match these definitions with the correct expressions.

1) a bank with physical branches
2) all day, every day of the week
3) a method of coding data to make it secure to transmit online
4) stealing somebody's personal and bank account details
5) a method of using a mobile phone to keep and spend money
6) someone who does not have the possibility to use banking services

a ☐ the unbanked
b ☐ mobile banking / mobile wallet
c ☐ encryption
d ☐ 24/7
e ☐ identity theft
f ☐ bricks and mortar bank / traditional bank

Unit 3 Business Banking

Listening

6 Listen to this report on the changes to High Street banks in the UK and choose the correct option.

1) What do people find annoying nowadays when making a bank transaction?
   A   A long queue.
   B   The remote location of the bank.
   C   A bad Internet connection.

2) Over the last two years, the number of people using High Street bank branches has continued
   A   to drop.
   B   to remain stable.
   C   to increase.

3) Which one is not a result of this change in the number of visitors?
   A   Many branches have closed down.
   B   Cashiers have found other jobs in the banking sector.
   C   Some areas no longer have a bank.

4) How have physical bank branches changed?
   A   There are more members of staff.
   B   There is more technology for customers.
   C   The staff is friendlier towards customers.

7 Listen to the report again and decide if the sentences are true (*T*) or false (*F*).

	T	F
1) Nowadays many people rely on Internet and mobile banking.	☐	☐
2) Many customers still like dealing in cash and interacting with real people.	☐	☐
3) Many smaller towns and remote areas in the UK have no banks at all.	☐	☐
4) The self-service machines cannot be used to view your balance and statement.	☐	☐

Speaking

8 What kinds of banking operations can be carried out online? Talk together. Then discuss with your partner the advantages and disadvantages of e-banking.

Writing

9 Write a short essay (150–200 words) to introduce the convenience that e-banking has brought to our life.

Technical Terms

sole trader	专营商	investment scheme	投资计划
cash machine	自动提款机，自动柜员机	foreign currency account	存在国外的外币账户
direct debit	直接借记，直接付款	exchange rate	汇率
standing order	（客户给银行的）定期付款指令，按期付款委托书	commercial mortgage	商业抵押，商业贷款
bank transfer	银行转账	full amount upfront	全额预付
bank charge	银行手续费	Internet banking	网上银行
account statement	对账单；账户报表	bank statement	银行对账单
surplus fund	剩余资金，盈余资金	mobile banking	手机银行
		account balance	账户余额

Unit 3 Business Banking

UNIT 4
Types of Cards and Fraud

Learning Objectives

Upon completion of the unit, students will be able to:
- compare the advantages and disadvantages of different payment methods;
- give proper advice on cards for different groups of people;
- understand different forms of fraud and how to prevent them.

Unit 4 Types of Cards and Fraud

Starting Off

1 How can you pay for something without using cash? Talk together about the different methods in different countries and then read the text below to check your ideas. What are the differences between China and these countries in the text?

Most banks and other financial institutions issue different types of cards which can be used to withdraw money from a cash machine or to make payments without having to use cash.

In the UK, the use of these cards, for both small and large purchases, is extremely widespread and cash and cheques are now used less and less often. There have even been talks about **abolishing** cheques altogether due to the decrease in popularity and as they are an expensive and time-consuming transaction for banks.

In the USA, however, cheques are still a popular form of payment, together with both cash and cards.

There has also been a massive **surge** in the number of **contactless** payments made in both the UK and the USA.

Many credit and debit cards, as well as smartphones, smart watches and other **devices**, can be used to make contactless payments where users simply need to place their card or device near a reader at the POS **terminal**. Contactless payments normally have an **upper limit** as a form of protection, **currently** set at £30 in the UK, $25 in the US and €25 in Europe.

MY GLOSSARY

abolish	v.	废除，废止	**terminal**	n.	终端机
surge	n.	剧增，激增	**upper limit**		上限，最高限制
contactless	adj.	无接触的			
device	n.	设备；终端	**currently**	adv.	当前；一般地

Reading 1

Payment Methods

Paypal

It is a system for keeping all different methods of payment—such as debit and credit cards—in one place. It is widely used for buying and selling on the Internet, especially for sites like **eBay**, because it offers a secure payment system where no one is able to see your financial details.

Cash Point Card

This card is used to withdraw cash and access the other services at a cash machine.

It has to be used in conjunction with a PIN (Personal Identification Number).

Credit Card

Most credit cards today are "chip and PIN" cards where a client only needs to enter a PIN at the POS terminal in order to make a purchase. The credit cards with magnetic stripes which have to be **swiped** with the customer signing a screen or paper **receipt** are gradually being **phased out** as they offer less security. For online purchases it is usually necessary to enter the card holder's name, card number, expiry date and the CCV (card code **verification**) number.

Unlike a debit card, with a credit card the customer can pay off the debt to the card issuer at a later moment. The customer receives a monthly statement and can choose to pay off the whole balance immediately or in **instalments** with high interest rates applied. Used wisely, credit cards can give you more than a month's free credit, as well as other advantages such as protection for online purchases.

Unit 4   Types of Cards and Fraud   35

Debit Card

This type of card is often combined with a cash point card. The customer uses this card instead of cash to make purchases anywhere there is POS terminal, such as shops, **petrol stations** and restaurants. It is necessary for the customer to type in a PIN on a keypad and then the amount is immediately **deducted** from the customer's bank account. With this type of card, many **outlets** offer a "**cashback**" facility where a customer can withdraw cash together with their purchase.

Pre-Paid Card

This type of card works in a similar way to a pay-as-you-go mobile phone. An amount of money is loaded onto the card which can then be used in the same way as a regular debit or credit card. The advantage is that, as they are not linked to a bank account, there is no risk of going overdrawn or running up large debts. When the amount on the card has been used up, it is impossible to continue using the card until it has been **topped up**. The disadvantage is that sometimes the **providers** charge high costs for issuing or topping up these cards.

MY GLOSSARY

Paypal	n. 贝宝（全球最大的在线支付平台）		**petrol station**	加油站
eBay	n. 易趣网		**deduct**	v. 减去，扣除
swipe	v. 刷卡		**outlet**	n. 专卖店；直销店
receipt	n. 收据		**cashback**	n. 返现
phase out	逐步淘汰，逐步停止使用		**top up**	充值；加满
verification	n. 核实，验证，查证		**provider**	n. 供应商，提供商
instalment	n. （分期付款的）一期			

2 Match the features with the cards. Tick (√) in the corresponding box.

Features	Cash Point Card	Credit Card	Debit Card	Pre-Paid Card
1) has a PIN				
2) means you pay immediately				
3) means you pay later				
4) means you pay in advance				
5) can be used in a cash machine				
6) can be used online				
7) can be used to withdraw cash at a POS terminal				
8) can have very high costs				
9) is linked to a bank account				
10) charges interest				

3 Read the text and answer the questions below.

1) What should be entered when we use the credit card for online shopping?

2) How long of free credit can credit cards give you?

3) What are the advantages and disadvantages of the pre-paid card?

Speaking

4 In small groups, discuss the advantages and disadvantages of the types of cards in Reading 1. Then choose one or two types of cards for the following people.

1) a 17-year-old student, living at home, who does not have a bank account
2) a university student, living away from home, who has a student loan
3) a business woman who travels internationally for work
4) a retired factory worker who lives on a state pension, and only has minimal savings

Unit 4   Types of Cards and Fraud

Reading 2

Fraud

In this technological and digital age, being aware of **fraud** is essential for businesses and individuals alike since the increase in online services has also led to an increase in the number of **attempts** made to **cheat** individuals and companies out of their money. Several decades ago, the worry was over false banknotes in **circulation** or **forged** cheques, but now financial fraud and **scams** are carried out over the Internet or with the latest technology.

Phishing

This is one common way that **fraudsters** attempt to steal information like usernames, **passwords**, credit card and bank account details. Potential **victims** receive emails which appear to be from a **reputable** company, like a bank, Paypal, or an e-commerce website, saying, for example, that there is a problem with their account or a **delivery**. Worried about the consequences, the victims click on the link provided to confirm their personal details which then allows the **criminal** to steal the data. Text messages can be used in a similar way, as can phone calls, when someone **pretending** to be the police or a bank tries to convince you to **reveal** banking security details, such as passwords and PINs.

Card Cloning

Most users of credit or debit cards are conscious of the risk of card cloning so, for example, they do not let their cards out of sight when paying in a restaurant and only use reputable websites for online purchases. However, card cloning is not always as easy to prevent.

A skimmer—a device which copies the details from the magnetic strip on a card—can be **inserted** over the **card slot** on cash machines or other automatic payment machines, such as ticket machines at a railway station, and are often very difficult to **detect**. Together with a hidden camera to **capture** the PIN as it is entered, these skimmers can store hundreds of card details before they are detected.

Financial and Investment Scams

There seems no limit to the imagination of scammers when it comes to inventing ideas to try to **con** people out of their money: emails asking for help to transfer funds from a foreign country; phone calls from **fake** insurance companies asking to confirm the details of a **policy** for valuable items in your home; websites and **brochures** promising no-risk, high return investments. The victims of these scams are often the elderly or those with little financial **expertise**, but even experienced investors and business people have been **taken in** by skilled scammers.

MY GLOSSARY

fraud	n.	欺骗; 骗子; 诡计
attempt	n.	尝试; 试图, 企图
cheat	v.	欺骗
circulation	n.	传播, 流通; 循环
forged	adj.	伪造的; 锻造的
scam	n.	欺诈, 骗局
	v.	欺诈, 诓骗
phishing	n.	网络欺骗
fraudster	n.	骗子
password	n.	密码; 口令
victim	n.	受害人; 牺牲者
reputable	adj.	声誉好的; 受尊敬的
delivery	n.	交付; 递送
criminal	n.	罪犯, 犯罪分子
pretend	v.	假装, 伪装
reveal	v.	透露; 泄露
insert	v.	插入, 嵌入
card slot		卡槽
detect	v.	察觉, 发现; 探测
capture	v.	捕捉; 拍摄
con	v.	欺骗, 哄骗
fake	adj.	假的, 冒充的
policy	n.	保险单; 政策
brochure	n.	小册子
expertise	n.	专门知识; 专家的意见
take in		欺骗

5 Read the text and decide if the sentences below are true (*T*) or false (*F*). If there is not enough information, choose "doesn't say" (*DS*).

		T	F	DS
1)	The aim of phishing is to get people to reveal private and confidential data.	☐	☐	☐
2)	Phishing techniques can also be used in text messages and phone calls.	☐	☐	☐
3)	The majority of card cloning is carried out when paying by credit card in a restaurant.	☐	☐	☐

4) It may not be easy to tell if a cash machine has been tampered with. ☐ ☐ ☐
5) Real insurance companies may want to check your policy details over the phone. ☐ ☐ ☐
6) Expert business people are never deceived by Internet investment scams. ☐ ☐ ☐

6 Match these words with the correct definitions.

1) fraud — a ☐ to trick somebody or make him/her believe something that is not true
2) cheat — b ☐ to take something from a person, shop, etc. without permission and without intending to return it or pay for it
3) forge — c ☐ the crime of getting money by deceiving people
4) scam — d ☐ to make an illegal copy
5) phishing — e ☐ the activity of copying the data of a credit card and using it illegally
6) steal — f ☐ a clever and dishonest plan for making money
7) cloning — g ☐ to trick somebody, especially in order to get money from him/her or persuade him/her to do something for you
8) con — h ☐ the activity of tricking people by getting them to give their identity, bank account numbers, etc. over the Internet or by email, and then using these to steal money from them

Listening

7 Listen to the recording about how to protect yourself from fraud and scams and fill in the gaps.

Credit card fraud
- Only use your credit card with (1) _____ and reputable sites.
- Check security by looking for the padlock icon and (2) _____ software.
- Check credit card (3) _____ carefully and then shred them.

Internet scams
- Always be (4) _____ of online offers.
- Do not reply to offers contained in (5) _____ emails.
- Do a background check on the company to see if it is (6) _____.

Business fraud
- Use (7) _____ sites for your online purchases.
- Check the (8) _____ of sellers on auction sites.
- Avoid companies that refuse to give you their (9) _____ or other details.

Writing

8 Write a short essay (150–200 words) describing the types of fraud that are carried out on the Internet.

Technical Terms

chip and PIN	芯片密码付款系统
magnetic stripe	磁条, 磁片
expiry date	到期日; 有效期限
pre-paid card	预付卡

Unit 4   Types of Cards and Fraud

UNIT 5 Payment Methods (1)

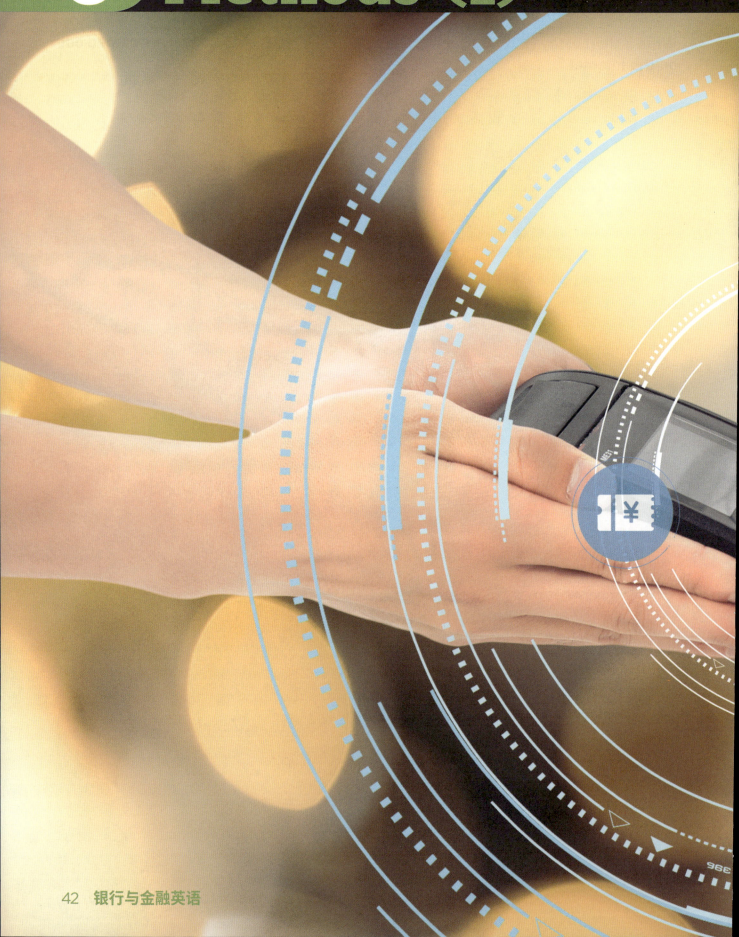

Learning Objectives

Upon completion of the unit, students will be able to:

- get familiar with the risks and benefits of international payment methods;
- know what information is necessary in a bank transfer;
- understand how a bill of exchange is useful in international trade.

Unit 5   Payment Methods (1)

Starting Off

1 How can buyers and sellers in international trade minimise payment risks? Read the text to check your ideas.

One of the biggest risks with international trade is payment, especially when dealing with new clients or a new market. Ideally, an **exporter** would like payment as soon as an order has been placed or before the goods are **dispatched**. On the other hand, an **importer** would prefer to **delay** payment at least until the goods have been received if not until they have been resold in order to generate **sufficient** income. This means that payment methods which are more secure for the exporter are riskier for the importer and **vice versa**. In order to find an **appropriate** payment method, the seller must first research the market and local trading conditions, including the economic and political situation, as well as the importer's credit standing. Then it is possible for the seller to balance his risks against customer requirements or expectations and to **negotiate** the most desirable method for both parties.

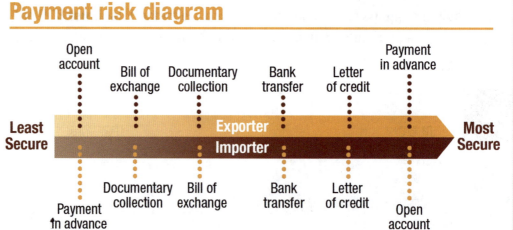

Payment risk diagram

MY GLOSSARY

exporter	n.	出口商; 输出国	sufficient	adj.	足够的, 充足的
dispatch	v.	发货; 发送, 派遣	vice versa		反之亦然
importer	n.	进口商; 输入国	appropriate	adj.	适当的, 恰当的, 合适的
delay	v.	延期, 延迟	negotiate	v.	谈判; 商议

Reading 1

Payment Conditions

Open Account

With an open account, the seller is extending credit to the buyer as goods and documents are shipped and delivered before payment is **due**, which is usually agreed to take place within 30, 60 or 90 days of the **invoice** date. Given that the goods are received in advance of any payment, it is obviously the most advantageous option for the buyer and the least secure for the seller. For this reason these conditions are normally only granted to **established** clients, with a favourable payment history and that are considered to be **creditworthy**. Regular customers may be offered credit on a **periodic** basis, such as **quarterly**, in which case the seller will send a statement of account with details of the transactions of that period and any amounts owing.

Payment in Advance

At the other end of the scale is payment in advance, the most secure for the seller, which **involves** taking payment before goods are dispatched. However, it is not widely used in international trade because buyers rarely accept this type of condition. There are two methods which are mainly used for small orders or new customers:

CWO (Cash with Order) The buyer pays in full at the moment of placing the order, usually by bank transfer as it is so immediate.

COD (Cash on Delivery) The goods are paid for when a carrier delivers them and the invoice to the buyer's door, otherwise they are not released.

MY GLOSSARY

due	adj.	应付的; 到期的
invoice	n.	发票; 发货单
established	adj.	资深的, 老牌的
creditworthy	adj.	(人或公司)信用可靠的
periodic	adj.	定期的; 周期的
quarterly	adj.	按季度的
at the other end of the scale		完全相反的情况是
involve	v.	包含; 涉及

Unit 5　Payment Methods (1)

2 Read the text and decide if the sentences are true (*T*) or false (*F*).

	T	F
1) Both open accounts and payments in advance are the least secure forms of payment for exporters.	☐	☐
2) An open account is a form of credit given by the seller to the buyer.	☐	☐
3) It is very unlikely that a new client will be given open account terms.	☐	☐
4) With payment in advance, the buyer is in a more secure position than the seller.	☐	☐
5) CWO means that the seller receives the customer's payment together with the order.	☐	☐
6) With COD, a buyer can take delivery of the goods and then pay for them.	☐	☐

Reading 2

Bank Transfer

A bank transfer, also called wire transfer, bank giro credit or credit transfer, is the most frequent and quickest system for international payments. The buyer instructs his bank to transfer the **relevant** sum of money directly from his bank account to the seller's bank account. The process is secure and fast for both parties involved. The information in a bank transfer includes: the names of the issuing and **beneficiary** banks, the buyer's and the seller's bank accounts, the currency, the amount to be transferred and usually a **reference** to the invoice number to make it easier for the seller to **trace** the details in his bank statement. The two banks involved will normally charge fees for the service, and sometimes if **intermediary** banks are used in the process, they will also demand payment for their involvement.

Common Acronyms

IBAN stands for "International Bank Account Number". This is a code of up to 34 **alphanumeric** characters which identify the country (using the ISO 3166-1 alpha-2 country codes), the bank, the branch and the account number where a transfer is to be made. IBANs are used in Europe and other countries around the world.

Whatever code system is used, the information must be supplied and entered into the system correctly to ensure the completion of the transfer.

SWIFT stands for "Society for Worldwide Interbank Financial Telecommunications". This organisation provides a network for secure communications between banks around the world. Each bank connected to the system has a unique code made up of 8 to 11 alphanumeric characters, commonly called a BIC (Bank Identifier Code) code.

MY GLOSSARY

relevant	adj.	相关的; 切题的
beneficiary	n.	受益者, 受益人
reference	n.	证明书; 参考, 参照
trace	v.	追溯, 追踪
intermediary	adj.	中间的, 媒介的
	n.	中间人
acronym	n.	首字母缩略词
alphanumeric	adj.	字母数字的

3 Read the text and complete the sentences below.

1) _____ are most commonly made by bank transfer.
2) The money _____ from the importer's bank account to the exporter's.
3) The issuing bank is _____ while the beneficiary bank is _____.
4) The bank transfer usually contains the invoice number so that _____.
5) Both the buyer and the seller will have to pay _____.
6) SWIFT and IBAN are _____ which are used to indicate the precise bank, branch or account number for a transfer.

Unit 5 Payment Methods (1) 47

4 Read the example below of a bank transfer confirmation, and then fill in the blanks.

Wire Transfer Payment Details Confirmation

Amount: 5,500
Currency: GBP
Country: UNITED KINGDOM

Beneficiary details
Beneficiary: John Smith Ltd.
Country: UNITED KINGDOM
Address: 7 Gresham Street, London W1
IBAN: GB14LOYD30943111644874

Beneficiary institution
SWIFT: LOYDGB21037
Beneficiary bank: LLOYDS TSB BANK PLC.
Country: UNITED KINGDOM

Additional information
Payment details: Ref. invoice No. 569 of 17 November 20..

☑ **Yes, I confirm** that all information that I have entered is correct and I accept all charges for this payment, including extra fees charged in case provided information is not correct.

1) the amount due _____
2) the currency _____
3) the name and country of the seller's bank _____
4) what the payment refers to _____

5 Choose the correct option to complete this email.

From: j.kinear@dabson.com
To: g.mason@hstores.com
Date: 11 August
Subject: Your order

Dear Mr Mason,

Thank you for your order no. 352/8 dated 10 August for our healthcare supplements. We are (1)___ to confirm that all the goods are in stock and will be dispatched on receipt of (2)___ of the total amount of £1,254.

Payment can be made by bank (3)___ to the following (4)___:

Account holder: Dabson Ltd
Bank: UBL
Branch: Leicester City Centre
Account (5)___: 0025698471
SWIFT   UBLBGB96807

We thank you once again for your order and look (6)___ to doing more business together in the future.

Yours sincerely,

Janice Kinear
Dabson Ltd

	A	B	C	D
1)	welcome	pleased	sure	satisfied
2)	payment	payable	paid	pay
3)	wire	credit	transfer	advance
4)	account	balance	credit	current
5)	currency	beneficiary	order	number
6)	up	forward	down	through

6 Reorder this dialogue between Mr Mason and a bank clerk.

- A ☐ A bank transfer? OK. Who is the beneficiary?
- B ☐ It's £1,254. I'd like it to be credited to their account tomorrow. Is that possible?
- A ☐ OK. That will be fine. And what is the amount?
- B ☐ Hello, this is Greg Mason from HStore. I need to make a bank transfer.
- A ☐ Good morning, Susan Pymm speaking.
- B ☐ No, but I've got the account number and SWIFT.
- A ☐ Have you done business with them before?
- B ☐ It's Dabson Ltd.
- A ☐ Yes. I'll take the details now, but you'll need to send an email or fax to confirm everything.
- B ☐ No it's the first time.
- A ☐ Have you got the IBAN?

Unit 5   Payment Methods (1)

Speaking

7 **Discuss these questions with a partner.**

1) Why do you think bank transfers are so widely used by businesses?
2) Do you think they are also common for private banking customers? Why / Why not?
3) Can you think of any situations when bank transfers are useful for private individuals?

Reading 3

Bill of Exchange

A bill of exchange (B/E), also known as a draft, is a written unconditional order by one party to another to pay a certain sum at a future date. The parties involved are:

- the **drawer**—the person or company who issues the draft;
- the **drawee**—the person or company that receives the draft and pays the sum **indicated**;
- the **payee**—the person or company that receives the money. Normally the payee and drawer are the same.

The time when the payment must be made—the **maturity** of the B/E—can be indicated in different ways:

- at sight / on demand, which means it can be **cashed** immediately;
- a fixed date indicating the exact date when it can be cashed;
- a term, such as 30/60/90 days, which means it can be cashed only after this period has passed.

| The drawer draws a B/E and sends it to the drawee. | The drawee accepts and **validates** the B/E by signing it and then returns it to the drawer. | The drawer sends the goods and passes the B/E to his bank. | The drawer's bank **forwards** the B/E to the drawee's bank. | The drawee's bank presents the bill for payment. |

```
                          BILL OF EXCHANGE
No. 37/B
For  £1,540.00                                    Date: 15 MARCH 20..
At   60 DAYS        After sight pay this First of Exchange (Second unpaid)
to the Order of  RAMSEY FURNITURE LTD.
the sum of  ONE THOUSAND FIVE HUNDRED AND FORTY POUNDS ONLY
Value  OF INVOICE NO. 528 OF 15 MARCH 20..

To                   on behalf of                    Accepted  John Walsh
H.J.W. BANK          RAMSEY FURNITURE LTD.           PETERBOROUGH LIMITED
35 MAIN STREET,      26 BLACKHALL ROAD, COVENTRY     87 GALWAY ROAD,
COVENTRY, UK         John Ramsey                     DUBLIN, IRELAND
```

A B/E is useful in international trade as it can be used as a form of credit because, being a negotiable document, it can be passed on to a third party if it is **endorsed** with the payee's **signature** on the back.

MY GLOSSARY

drawer	n. 出票人, 开票人	**cash**	v. 将……兑现; 支付现款
drawee	n. 付款人, 受票人	**validate**	v. 证实, 验证; 确认; 使生效
indicate	v. 指出, 表明	**forward**	v. 发送; 转寄; 促进; 运送
payee	n. 领款人, 收款人	**endorse**	v. 背书, 在背面签字
maturity	n. 到期日	**signature**	n. 签字, 签名

8 Read the text and choose the correct alternative.

1) A B/E involves a *maximum / minimum* of two parties.
2) The maturity of a bill of exchange is *when / where* the bill can be cashed.
3) A *term / sight* draft can be cashed immediately.
4) To be valid, a B/E *has to / does not have to* be signed by the drawee.
5) A B/E is a *non-negotiable / negotiable* document.

9 Look at the B/E above and answer these questions.

1) What is the name of the drawer of the B/E?

_____

2) Who is the drawee?

_____

3) What is the amount of the B/E?

4) What is its maturity?

5) What is the date of issue?

10 Paraphrase the following words and expressions.

1) B/E or draft
2) drawer
3) drawee
4) maturity
5) at sight
6) term
7) negotiable document
8) endorsed

Writing

11 Write a short essay (150–200 words) on the different methods of payments presented in this unit. Include the following points:

- how each method works;
- the benefits for the buyer and the seller;
- the risks for the buyer and the seller.

Technical Terms

credit standing	信用状况; 商业信誉
extending credit	信贷展期
wire transfer	电汇
bank giro credit	银行转账信贷
credit transfer	信用转账
bill of exchange	汇票
at sight / on demand	即期付款
negotiable document	可转让单据; 流通单据

Unit 5 Payment Methods (1)

UNIT 6　Payment Methods (2)

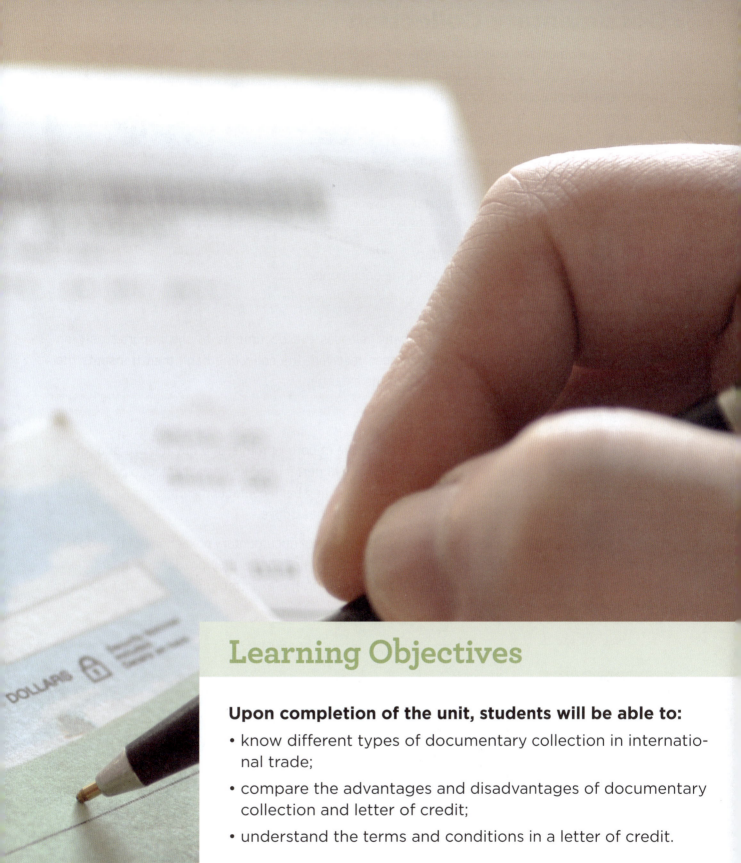

Learning Objectives

Upon completion of the unit, students will be able to:
- know different types of documentary collection in international trade;
- compare the advantages and disadvantages of documentary collection and letter of credit;
- understand the terms and conditions in a letter of credit.

Unit 6 Payment Methods (2)

Reading 1

Documentary Collection

With documentary collection, the exporter presents the shipping documents, invoice and bill of exchange to his bank (the **remitting** bank) when the goods are ready for shipping. The remitting bank forwards all the documents to the importer's bank (the collecting bank), which will release them to the importer giving him ownership of the goods.

There are two types of documentary collection which determine the release of the documents:

Documents Against Payment (D/P)

With this method, the collecting bank releases the documents to the importer only on payment of the B/E. Once payment has been received, the collecting bank then **transmits** the funds to the remitting bank for payment to the exporter.

Documents Against Acceptance (D/A)

This method represents a form of credit as the importer promises to pay the B/E at a future date. The collecting documents are released to the importer once he has accepted to pay the B/E on a specified date. At maturity of the B/E, the collecting bank contacts the importer for payment and will then transfer the funds to the remitting bank as above.

The two banks act as intermediaries in the process of documentary collection but they do not **verify** that the documents conform to the contract of sale, nor do they provide any guarantees. This method of payment is fairly advantageous for both the exporter and the importer and it is less risky than an open account.

MY GLOSSARY

remit	v. 汇款；免除（债务或处罚）	transmit	v. 转寄
		verify	v. 核实；查证

1 Read the text and decide if the sentences below are true (*T*) or false (*F*). If there is not enough information, choose "doesn't say" (*DS*).

	T	F	DS
1) Both the importer's bank and the exporter's bank are involved in documentary collection.	☐	☐	☐
2) A bill of exchange is not a compulsory part of this method of payment.	☐	☐	☐
3) The shipping and other documents must be prepared in triplicate.	☐	☐	☐
4) With D/P, ownership of the goods passes to the buyer once the B/E has been paid.	☐	☐	☐
5) With D/A, the buyer has more time to pay for the goods than with D/P.	☐	☐	☐
6) The banks involved offer guarantees for the transaction.	☐	☐	☐

Speaking

2 Discuss these questions in pairs.

1) What are the similarities and differences between documentary collection and cash on delivery?
2) How is D/A similar to an open account? Does it offer more or less guarantees to the exporter?
3) What differences are there between documentary collection and a bill of exchange? Which method is more secure? Why?

Unit 6   Payment Methods (2)   57

Reading 2

Documentary Letter of Credit

A letter of credit (L/C) is a **contractual** agreement in which the importer's bank guarantees that payment will be made to the exporter provided that the terms and conditions stated in the L/C have been met, that is if the requested documents have been presented and are in order. It is one of the most **secure** methods of payment available to international traders, especially in new or recently established business relationships or when it is difficult to obtain details of the **creditworthiness** of an exporter. The importer is secure since the bank must verify the documents and payment is made after shipment; the exporter is secure in that he will receive payment as long as the documents he provides are in order. This last point may represent a disadvantage of this form of payment in so much that any **discrepancy** between the L/C and the documents presented could mean expensive **amendments** or even non-payment. The high bank costs, usually entirely born by the importer, are another **drawback** to this method and means it is not suitable for small sums.

> The typical documents requested include the following, often requested in **duplicate** or **triplicate**: commercial invoice, clean bill of lading, insurance policy, packing list and Certificate of Origin.

The main parties involved are the importer (**applicant**), the exporter (beneficiary), the importer's bank (issuing bank) and the exporter's bank (advising bank) and the basic procedure for a L/C can be broken down into these nine steps:

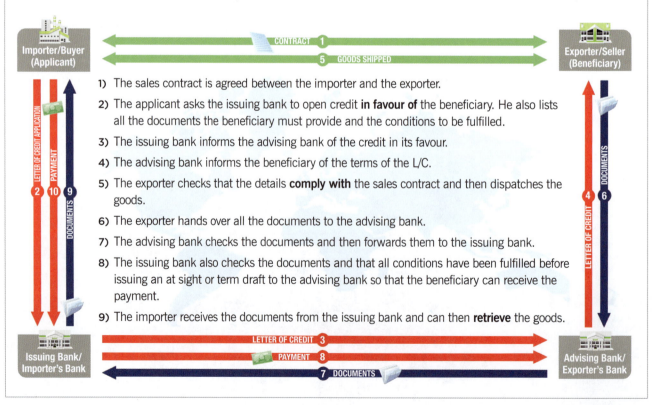

1) The sales contract is agreed between the importer and the exporter.
2) The applicant asks the issuing bank to open credit **in favour of** the beneficiary. He also lists all the documents the beneficiary must provide and the conditions to be fulfilled.
3) The issuing bank informs the advising bank of the credit in its favour.
4) The advising bank informs the beneficiary of the terms of the L/C.
5) The exporter checks that the details **comply with** the sales contract and then dispatches the goods.
6) The exporter hands over all the documents to the advising bank.
7) The advising bank checks the documents and then forwards them to the issuing bank.
8) The issuing bank also checks the documents and that all conditions have been fulfilled before issuing an at sight or term draft to the advising bank so that the beneficiary can receive the payment.
9) The importer receives the documents from the issuing bank and can then **retrieve** the goods.

MY GLOSSARY

contractual	*adj.* 合同的, 契约的	drawback	*n.*	缺点, 不利条件
duplicate	*adj.* 复制的; 二重的	applicant	*n.*	申请人, 申请者, 请求者
triplicate	*adj.* 一式三份的; 三联的			
secure	*adj.* 安全的	in favour of		有利于; 支持, 赞同
creditworthiness	*n.* 信誉; 信用可靠程度	comply with		照做, 遵守
discrepancy	*n.* 不符; 矛盾; 相差	retrieve	*v.*	取回, 找回
amendment	*n.* 附加条款; 改善, 改正			

3 Read the text and answer the questions below.

1) In what kind of situation is a letter of credit advisable?

_____

2) What information does a letter of credit contain?

_____

3) What documents are usually necessary?

_____

4) Who are the parties involved?

_____

4 Complete this table with the advantages and disadvantages of a letter of credit.

Advantages	
Disadvantages	

Unit 6   Payment Methods (2)

5 Who is responsible for the following steps: the applicant, the beneficiary, the issuing bank or the advising bank? Fill in the blanks.

1) deciding the conditions and documents to include _____
2) opening the credit in favour of the beneficiary _____
3) notifying the beneficiary of the L/C _____
4) dispatching the goods _____
5) giving the documents to the advising bank _____
6) checking the documents _____
7) issuing a draft to the advising bank _____
8) claiming the goods from the freight company _____

Reading 3

Example of Letter of Credit

HSBC–BRISTOL ORIGINAL

Advising bank: BANK OF CHINA, QINGDAO, CHINA
Form of doc. credit: IRREVOCABLE
Doc. credit number: 89578965
Date of issue: 12 01 20.. (01 Dec 20..)
Expiry: Date: 02 16 20.. (16 Feb 20..)
Place: PEOPLE'S REP. OF CHINA

****Amount****
USD****35,000.00

Applicant:
JONES FOOTWEAR
25 HIGH STREET
BRISTOL
UK

Beneficiary:
XINGZHOU IMPORT & EXPORT CO. LTD.
SHANGHAI SOUTH ROAD 2754
QINGDAO
CHINA

Available with: HSBC BRISTOL
Deferred payment: 60 DAYS AFTER BILL OF LADING DATE
Partial shipments: NOT ALLOWED
Transhipments: NOT ALLOWED
Port of loading: QINGDAO PORT (PEOPLE'S REP. OF CHINA)
Port of discharge: PORTSMOUTH (UK)
Latest date of shipment: 01 31 20.. (31 Jan 20..)
Description of goods: 35,000 PAIRS OF FLIP FLOPS AS PER PRO-FORMA INVOICE No. 4859 DD 15 OCT 20.. AMOUNTING TO TOTAL USD 35,000.00 FOR GOODS RENDERED CIF PORTSMOUTH (UK)

An L/C is normally **irrevocable** which means that it cannot be changed unless both parties agree.

A revocable L/C is also possible, although it is not recommended since it allows the applicant to make changes without the **consent** of the beneficiary. The beneficiary may ask that the L/C is confirmed by the advising bank. This is called a confirmed L/C and it means that the advising bank guarantees to pay if the issuing bank fails to do so. A confirmed irrevocable L/C offers the maximum protection to the exporter.

Documents required:	1) FULL SET OF CLEAN "ON BOARD" MARINE BILL OF LADING ISSUED TO ORDER AND BLANK ENDORSED, MARKED "FREIGHT PREPAID", NOTIFY APPLICANT. 2) SIGNED COMMERCIAL INVOICE, 2 ORIGINALS + 2 COPIES, DULY DATED STATING THAT INVOICED AND SHIPPED GOODS COMPLY IN EVERY RESPECT WITH THE ONES DESCRIBED IN PRO-FORMA INVOICE No. 4859 DD 15 OCT. 20.. 3) PACKING LIST, 2 ORIGINALS + 2 COPIES 4) CERTIFICATE OF ORIGIN "FORM A", ORIGINAL + 1 COPY, ISSUED BY COMPETENT AUTHORITIES IN PEOPLE'S REP. OF CHINA, STATING GOODS OF ORIGIN OF: PEOPLE'S REP. OF CHINA 5) INSURANCE POLICY COVERING ALL RISKS FOR 110 PCT OF INVOICE VALUE, ORIGINAL + 1 COPY
Additional conditions:	L/C AMOUNT COVERS 100 PCT (%) OF INVOICE VALUE
Details of charges:	ALL BANKING COMMISSIONS AND CHARGES OUT OF ARE TO BNF'S ACCOUNT
Presentation period:	DOCS TO BE PRESENTED WITHIN 16 DAYS AFTER BILL OF LADING DATE
Confirmation:	WITHOUT

MY GLOSSARY

irrevocable		*adj.*	不可改变的; 不能取消的	**partial shipment**		分批装运; 部分装运
consent		*n.*	同意, 允许	**transhipment**	*n.*	转运
defer		*v.*	延期, 推迟			

6 Read the letter of credit on the previous page and answer these questions.

1) Is it irrevocable?

2) Is it confirmed?

3) What is the total amount of the letter of credit?

4) Is payment due at sight or term?

5) What documents have been requested?

6) Who will pay the bank charges?

Unit 6   Payment Methods (2)

7 Match these terms with the correct definitions.

1) exporter   a ☐ a formal agreement to accept responsibility for something
2) importer   b ☐ a person or organisation that coordinates financial and business transactions between two companies
3) invoice   c ☐ a person or business that buys goods from another country to sell
4) intermediary d ☐ the state of having enough money or property in order to be given a loan or credit
5) ownership   e ☐ a difference between two things which should be the same
6) guarante   f ☐ a document with details of the buyer, seller, goods or services and amount to be paid
7) creditworthiness g ☐ the right or state of being the owner
8) discrepancy h ☐ a person or business that sells goods to another country

Listening

8 Listen to a conversation and fill in the blanks with the words you hear.

A: Good morning, sir. Is there anything I can do for you?

B: Yes, I think so. My purpose of coming here is to ask you to (1) _____ for my company.

A: Well, what kind of L/C?

B: We have just concluded a transaction. We'll import 300 sets of textile machines from Germany. The German side requires (2) _____.

A: I see. What is (3) _____?

B: It's ￥1,800,000.

A: (4) _____! We have to check the balance of your account first.

B: By the way, if you open this L/C for us, our (5) _____, that is to say, some clauses will be altered, for example, the time of delivery and L/C will be a distance one, not at sight. Can we amend it? Is it complicated?

A: Yes, you can apply to amend it. Well, it's not very complicated, but you need to fill in one (6) _____ and pay for it.

B: I see.

A: For settling through L/C, you should be very careful, (7) _____, because even one small mistake will cause you a great loss.

B: Exactly, thank you.

Writing

9 Write a short essay (150–200 words) on documentary collection and letter of credit, explaining the advantages and drawbacks for both the importer and the exporter.

Technical Terms

documentary collection	跟单托收
remitting bank	寄单行; 汇出行
collecting bank	代收银行
document against payment (D/P)	付款交单
document against acceptance (D/A)	承兑交单
documentary letter of credit	跟单信用证
bill of lading	提货单
deferred payment	延期付款

Unit 6 Payment Methods (2) 63

UNIT 7
Stock Exchanges and Commodity Exchanges

Learning Objectives

Upon completion of the unit, students will be able to:
- know the key concepts related to stock exchanges;
- explain the role of commodity exchanges in the trade of futures contracts;
- understand the role of a broker;
- know the history and development of London and New York Stock Exchanges.

Unit 7   Stock Exchanges and Commodity Exchanges

Starting Off

1 Is there a stock exchange in China? What is it called? Can you think of other stock exchanges? Talk together.

Reading 1

A stock exchange is a regulated financial market where **securities**, such as shares and bonds, are bought and sold. It has two functions:

- in the primary market it helps companies raise capital by selling shares, for example through an IPO (initial public offering);
- in the secondary market it acts as an intermediary between those wishing to sell and those wanting to buy shares.

In some stock exchanges trading is still carried out in a traditional manner with the **brokers** on the trading floor, shouting out orders and instructions. Most, however, have moved completely or at least partially to using online and phone trading. Trading can only be carried out by members. Share prices can naturally go both up and down (bear and bull markets), depending on market forces of supply and demand as well as other factors such as positive or negative industry and company reports and forecasts. Naturally, the purpose of anyone trading on the stock exchange is to make a profit by buying low and selling high.

A commodity exchange, also referred to as **futures** market or futures exchange, is where various commodities and **derivatives** (financial products that have a value based on that of another asset) are traded. Some of the biggest commodity exchanges are located in Chicago, USA, divided according to the commodities and other financial instruments they deal in. Commodity exchanges act as intermediaries in the

> A bond is an instrument of debt, issued by governments and companies, where the bond issuer pays a fixed rate of interest to the bond holder for the life of the bond until its maturity, when the value of the bond is also repaid.
>
> A bull market is when there is confidence in the market and share prices are generally rising. A bear market, on the other hand, is when prices are **predicted** to fall.

trade of futures contracts, commonly known as futures. These are agreements to buy or sell a certain quantity of a commodity at a **predetermined** price and date. By attempting to predict price movements, the seller wants to fix the best possible rate, protecting himself against future price drops, while the buyer wishes to avoid any future price increases.

MY GLOSSARY

securities	n. 有价证券	futures	n. 期货	
broker	n. 经纪人, 掮客	derivative	n. 金融衍生产品	
predict	v. 预言, 预知; 预报; 断言	predetermine	v. 预先决定, 预先确定, 事先安排	

2 Read the text and decide if the sentences below are true (*T*) or false (*F*). If there is not enough information, choose "doesn't say" (*DS*).

	T	F	DS
1) Shares are bought and sold on the primary market.	☐	☐	☐
2) The primary market is not as big as the secondary market.	☐	☐	☐
3) Bull market and bear market indicate two opposing trends in share prices.	☐	☐	☐
4) Trading can be carried out electronically and face-to-face.	☐	☐	☐
5) Positive or negative information regarding a company can affect its share price.	☐	☐	☐
6) Commodity exchanges are in the same place as stock exchanges.	☐	☐	☐
7) Futures are contracts where the price of the commodity is fixed in the future.	☐	☐	☐
8) Futures help protect against upward and downward changes in price.	☐	☐	☐

Speaking 1

3 In pairs, explain the role of commodity exchanges in the trade of futures contracts.

Unit 7   Stock Exchanges and Commodity Exchanges

Reading 2

Indices

An **index** is an indicator of trends on the stock exchange which can provide a quick picture of what is happening. A **portfolio** of stocks, traded on a particular exchange, are selected to represent a particular market or investment area. When an index goes up, it basically means that there are more people buying than selling and share prices have risen. The index goes down when people are **dumping** shares.

Charles Dow is credited with the first share index when he created the Dow industrial average in 1886. Today it is known as the Dow Jones Industrial Average (DJIA) or just Dow Jones and is based on 30 **blue-chip** companies quoted on the NYSE. Two other well-known indices are the Financial Times Stock Exchange 100 and the Nasdaq 100. The former—also known as Footsie for short—is an index that measures the share price **performance** of the one hundred largest, most actively traded companies on the London Stock Exchange. The Nasdaq 100 Index includes over one hundred of the largest domestic and international non-financial securities which are listed on the Nasdaq Stock Market in New York.

Spread

The general definition of spread is the difference between two prices or interest rates. In the stock market, it refers to the gap between the current **bid** and ask price of a share or other security, also known as bid/ask or bid/offer spread.

Bond spread is used when talking about the difference between **yields** of **comparable** bonds. To **gauge** the performance of a company or government bond, its yield is often compared to that of a **benchmark** bond, which carries less or no risk of **default**, such as the German Bund or US Treasury bonds. The wider the spread between the two bond yields, the greater the risk is.

Brokers

In order to be able to buy and sell shares on a stock exchange, it is necessary to go through an authorised broker who can trade on behalf of a customer. Brokers can be part of a bank or **brokerage** firm, both of which may also offer online trading at low rates for small and private investors. All brokers have to pass particular national exams and are regulated by bodies such as the FCA (Financial Conduct Authority) in the UK and the SEC (Security and Exchange Commission) in the USA. They earn their money by charging a **commission** on each transaction.

There are three types of brokers:

- **Execution** only: These brokers carry out a client's instructions to buy or sell shares but do not give any advice. This type of broker receives a lower commission rate.

- Advisory: These brokers provide advice, giving details of the current trends, analysis of shares and companies for example, and then execute the client's order to buy and sell.

- **Discretionary**: These brokers buy and sell shares based on a client's instructions, but they are also authorised to make investment decisions without having prior **approval** from the client. This type of broker will naturally work on a higher commission rate.

MY GLOSSARY

index	n.	指数；目录
portfolio	n.	证券投资组合
dump	v.	抛售；倾倒
blue-chip	adj.	（公司或投资）蓝筹的，可靠的
performance	n.	表现；绩效
bid	n.	出价；投标
yield	n.	利润，收益；产量
comparable	adj.	类似的，相当的，可比的
gauge	v.	（尤指用测量仪器）测量，计量，测算；判定，判断
benchmark	n.	基准
default	n.	拖欠；违约
brokerage	n.	经纪公司
commission	n.	佣金，服务费
execution	n.	实行，履行，执行
discretionary	adj.	任意的，自由决定的
approval	n.	允许，许可

Unit 7 Stock Exchanges and Commodity Exchanges

4 Read the text and answer these questions.

1) What is the purpose of an index?

2) What stock exchanges do the Dow Jones, FTSE 100 and Nasdaq 100 refer to?

3) What is the definition of spread?

4) What is the role of a broker?

5) What role do the FCA and SEC have for brokers?

6) Why does an execution-only broker earn less commission?

7) What is the difference between advisory and discretionary brokers?

Speaking 2

5 Discuss these questions in pairs.

1) What are the opportunities for working in a stock exchange or commodity exchange in China?
2) Are there national exams you have to take?
3) What do you think are the positive and negative aspects of being a broker?
4) Would you like to work as a broker? Why / Why not?

Reading 3

London Stock Exchange

The London Stock Exchange was founded in 1801 although its **origins** go back to the 17th century. Brokers would meet in Jonathan's Coffee House to discuss investments and trade in shares and a list of the prices of shares and commodities was created. From there a group of brokers formed a club, which in 1801 was opened on a formal basis.

Since 2004 the LSE has been situated in Paternoster Square, near St. Paul's Cathedral.

Key dates in the Exchange's history

1973:	female members were admitted for the first time
1986:	the deregulation of the market, known as the "Big Bang"
2000:	vote by shareholders to become a public limited company
2007:	merger with Borsa Italiana, creating the London Stock Exchange Group, Europe's leading diversified exchange business

The Big Bang was a change in the Stock Exchange's structure and operations. The Exchange became a private limited company. Trading **ceased** to be done face-to-face on the trading floor and screen-based electronic trading was introduced, using phones and computers. Fixed commission rates were abolished and all firms could operate as broker/dealers trading on behalf of clients and on their own account without the need for an intermediary.

Here is an example of **quotation** on magnetic tape or **ticker**:

MSFT ₅K @ 61.25 ▼ 1.35

↑ Ticker Symbol ↑ Shares Traded ↑ Price Traded ↑ Change Direction ↑ Change Amount

Ticker Symbol	The Unique Characters used to identify the company.
Shares Traded	The volume for the trade being quoted. Abbreviations are: K = 1,000, M = 1 million and B = 1 billion
Price Traded	The price per share for the articular trade (the last bid price).
Change Direction	Shows whether the stock is trading higher or lower than the previous day's closing price.
Change Amount	The difference in price from the previous day's close.

These symbols are usually in the following colours:
- Green indicates the stock is trading higher than the previous day's close.
- Red indicates the stock is trading lower than the previous day's close.
- Blue or white means the stock is unchanged from the previous closing price.

MY GLOSSARY

origin	n.	起源, 来源
quotation	n.	报价; 报价单
ticker	n.	（股票行情等的）自动收报机
cease	v.	停止, 中止, 中断

6 Read the text and complete the sentences below.

1) The London Stock Exchange started with _____.
2) Until 1973, there were no _____.
3) The purpose of the Big Bang was to _____.
4) The London Stock Exchange Group was created by _____.

Speaking 3

7 Ticker symbols are used to represent the companies quoted on a stock exchange. Can you work out what the companies are in this ticker tape? They are all quoted on the NYSE.

1	2	3	4	5	6
AMZN $_{2.8M@}$253.96s1.47	NOK$_{151M@}$3.88s0.44	AAPL$_{37M@}$538.79t37.05	MSFT$_{68M@}$26.67s0.30	MCD$_{5M@}$86.97t0.23	GOOG$_{1.8M@}$687.82t3.21

Reading 4

New York Stock Exchange

The New York Stock Exchange is the oldest and largest in the USA and is located on Wall Street. The beginnings of the Exchange can be traced back to 1792 when twenty-four brokers met under a tree in Wall Street and signed an agreement establishing the rules for buying and selling company shares. The NYSE is one of the few exchanges in the world that still operates using the traditional open **outcry** system, that is where the brokers meet face-to-

face on the trading floor, in addition to electronic trading. The NYSE became public in 2006. Prior to this it was a membership-only organisation and it was possible to join only by purchasing one of the existing 1,366 seats. A year later it merged with Euronext, the European combined stock market, and formed the NYSE Euronext, the first **transatlantic** stock exchange. In 2013, it was **acquired** by Intercontinental Exchange to create the **premier** financial markets operator. International Exchange also acquired the Chicago Stock Exchange in 2018.

Trading on the NYSE opens and closes with a bell ringing, which you can watch live on the Exchange's website at 9:30 a.m. for the opening bell and at 4 p.m. for the closing bell. Many famous people from actors and athletes to **politicians** and **entrepreneurs** have rung the bell.

MY GLOSSARY

outcry	n.	喊价; 大声呼喊
transatlantic	adj.	横渡大西洋的; 在大西洋彼岸的
acquire	v.	并购; 取得; 捕获
premier	adj.	第一的, 首要的
politician	n.	政治家, 政客
entrepreneur	n.	企业家

8 Read the text and complete the sentences below.

1) The NYSE trades by using both _____.
2) For most of its existence, the NYSE was a _____.
3) In 2006 the NYSE _____.
4) In 2013, NYSE _____.

Listening

9 Listen to this expert talking about stock market crashes and economic bubbles and choose the correct option.

1) Tulip Mania is an example of _____.

   A a good investment opportunity

Unit 7   Stock Exchanges and Commodity Exchanges

B an economic bubble

C how to invest in the Dutch Stock Exchange

2) Why did the price of tulip bulbs rise?

A There was a shortage of bulbs.

B They were used to trade instead of money.

C They were popular and in demand.

3) What happened after prices peaked?

A Bulb dealers started trading abroad.

B Bulb dealers imported other flowers.

C People lost a lot of money.

4) In the late 1990s, dot-com companies were quoted on the stock exchange even if _____.

A they had no profits

B they were newly founded companies

C people were not confident about their future

5) During this period, investors often invested _____.

A too much money in the same company

B without checking out the company thoroughly

C when the share price was already too high

6) What happened in March 2000?

A The dot-com companies failed to make a profit.

B The economic bubble burst.

C Trading in dot-com companies was interrupted.

Speaking 4

10 Prepare a short presentation (3–5 minutes) on share and securities trading and the risks involved, including:

- the difference between a stock exchange and a commodity exchange;
- the role of a broker;
- the importance of indices;
- fraud and speculation.

Writing

11 Write a short essay (150–200 words) introducing one stock exchange in China. Include the following points: when it was founded; scope of business and functions; its ranking in the world.

Technical Terms

initial public offering	首次公开发行
commodity exchange	商品交易所
bull market	牛市
bear market	熊市
Dow Jones Industrial Average	道琼斯工业平均指数
Financial Times Stock Exchange 100	金融时报100指数
Nasdaq 100	纳斯达克100指数
Financial Conduct Authority	金融行为监管局
Security and Exchange Commission	证券交易委员会
London Stock Exchange	伦敦证券交易所
Big Bang	股票交易改革
New York Stock Exchange	纽约证券交易所
Euronext	泛欧交易所; 欧洲证券交易所
NYSE Euronext	纽约泛欧证交所集团
Intercontinental Exchange	洲际交易所
Chicago Stock Exchange	芝加哥证券交易所

Unit 7 Stock Exchanges and Commodity Exchanges

UNIT 8 Explaining Financial Data

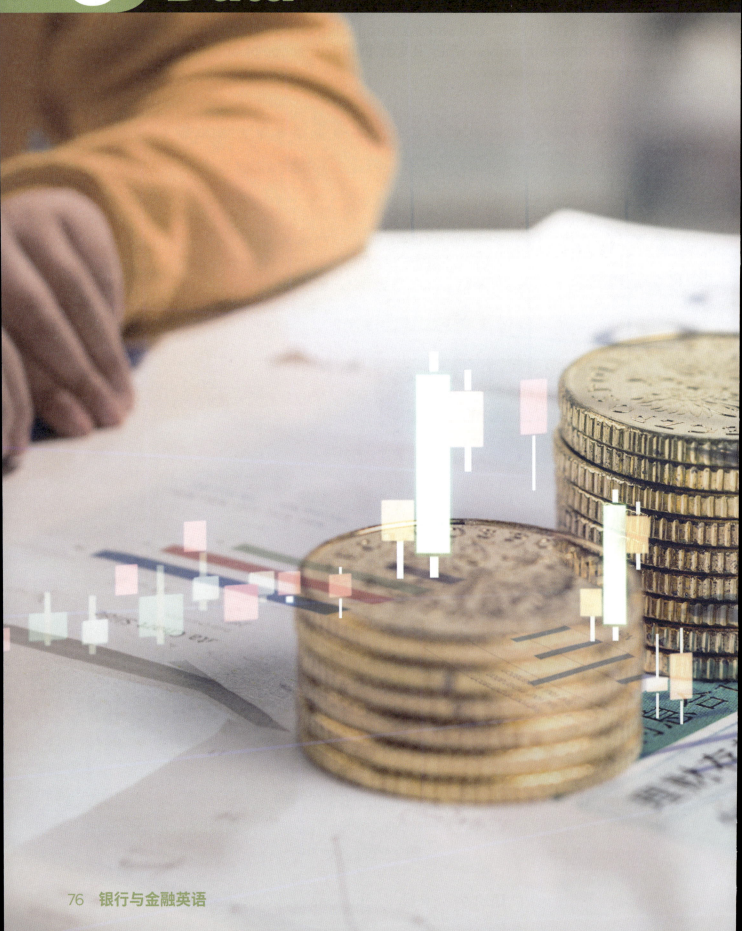

Learning Objectives

Upon completion of the unit, students will be able to:
- describe financial data through a chart;
- explain results, trends and forecasts on charts and graphs;
- master common verbs and adverbs that describe data changes.

Unit 8 Explaining Financial Data

Starting Off

1 What kind of financial information is often presented in graph form? Why? Discuss with your partner.

Reading

Newspapers, company annual reports, government papers and many other kinds of documents contain financial data, which is often presented in **graph** form, to show results, trends and **forecasts**. Think about indices like the FTSE 100 or Dow Jones, currency exchange rates, company performance  **statistics** with sales, expenditure and profits. The use of graphs makes the information **immediate** to see and easy to understand without having to read a lot of text. Any **accompanying** articles or reports usually go into more details, picking up on some of the **principal** figures to explain and analyse them **in depth**. It is a useful skill to be able to read this kind of graph, and **summarise** it both in written form and **orally**.

MY GLOSSARY

graph	n.	图表; 曲线图
forecast	n.	预测, 预报; 预想
statistic	n.	统计资料, 统计数据; 统计量
immediate	adj.	立即的, 直接的; 最接近的
accompanying	adj.	陪同的, 陪伴的
principal	adj.	主要的; 资本的
in depth		深入地; 全面地
summarise	v.	概括; 总结
orally	adv.	口头地; 口述地

2 Put these verbs into the correct column to indicate their meaning.

go up	increase	go down	decrease	fall	decline
grow	stabilise	drop	rise	improve	level off
peak	plummet	steady	jump	pick up	climb
become stable	soar	recover	rally	boom	dip
rocket	plunge	crash	remain constant		

↑	→	↓
rise,	level off,	plummet,

3 Look at the sentences on the left and complete their opposites by choosing the words and expressions in the box.

| has changed | rose | decrease | lowest ever rate | fell dramatically | have been lowered |

1) Sales grew rapidly in the first quarter. ⟷ Sales _____ in the first three months of the year.

2) Holiday prices reached a peak in July. ⟷ July saw holiday prices at their _____.

3) Oil prices have remained constant. ⟷ The price of oil _____.

4) There has been a 1% rise in interest rates. ⟷ Interest rates _____ by 1%.

5) Output has increased sharply this month. ⟷ There has been a significant _____ in output this month.

6) The price of mobile phones dropped by 9%. ⟷ Mobile phone prices _____ by 9%.

4 Match each sentence below with the correct graph and write it in each blank.

- Performance dropped twice during the period in question.
- After a stable beginning to the year, profits plummeted in May.
- After an initial period of fluctuation, share prices levelled off.
- Last year, sales peaked dramatically in the second quarter.
- The forecast is that both online and phone orders will decline in October.
- Over the four year period in question, sales increased steadily.

Unit 8   Explaining Financial Data   79

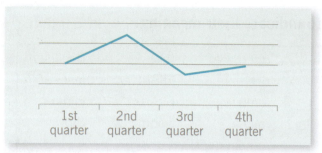

1) A _____
   B Then they *fell rapidly* between the second and third quarter, before _____ at the end of the year.

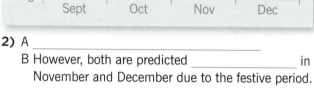

2) A _____
   B However, both are predicted _____ in November and December due to the festive period.

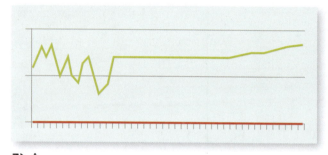

3) A _____
   B Towards the end of the period they began to _____.

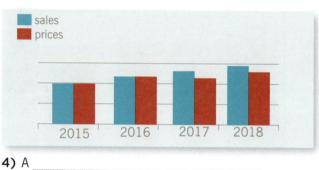

4) A _____
   B Prices also showed a similar, positive trend, although in 2017 they _____.

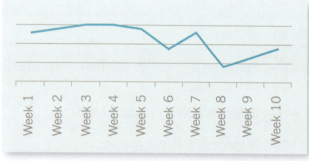

5) A _____
   B In fact, in week 8 it dropped sharply, before _____ again at the end of the 10 week period.

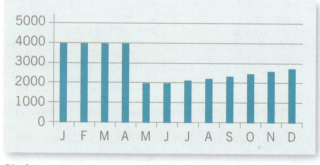

6) A _____
   B By December they had _____ but were still far below January's figures.

5 Use a verb from the table in Exercise 2 with an appropriate adverb from the list below to complete the second sentence under each graph in Exercise 4. Pay attention to the form of the verb. More than one answer is possible.

Speed of change: suddenly/sharply/quickly/rapidly/fast/steadily/gradually/gently/slowly/sluggishly

Amount of change: dramatically/significantly/considerably/markedly/slightly/fractionally/marginally

6 Choose the correct option to complete this summary of a day's trading in London.

London shares (1) _____ on Friday, continuing the strong gains which started on Tuesday's trading session. After jumping 2.3% on Thursday, the FTSE 100 index closed up 25.4 points or 0.39%. A(n) (2) _____ in commodity prices benefitted petroleum and energy companies, with Wickstead Oil closing up 4.04%.

Shares in TAL Right Brothers fell 4.98% after its (3) _____ third-quarter trading update. The company declared a(n) (4) _____ in sales volumes, thanks to growth in the Japanese market. However, revenues dropped (5) _____ 11% due to the depreciation of the Yen and other currencies against the US dollar.

In the FTSE 250, Halon shares (6) _____ 7.6% after the DIY chain reported a 3.8% rise in sales for the period from August to October. On the currency markets, the pound was (7) _____ against the euro and went up 0.75% to €1.2561 but (8) _____ 0.25% against the dollar, down to $1.5103.

1) A leveled off   B went down   C went up
2) A decrease   B increase   C drop
3) A exceptional   B outstanding C disappointing
4) A rise   B slump   C increase
5) A by   B from   C of
6) A plummeted   B crashed   C increased
7) A negative   B positive   C stable
8) A plunged   B soared   C fell

7 Look at the graph and complete this article with a suitable word for each gap.

TNP is a small nanotechnology company based near Cambridge and it has had a few mad days of trading on the London Stock Exchange. Shares had been (1) _____ before 22nd May and were (2) _____ for less than £3. They closed on Wednesday 26th May at about £22—an amazing (3) _____ of (4) _____ 1,000%. At one point on Tuesday TNP shares actually (5) _____ as high as £49.68, which meant the (6) _____ since 22nd May was 30,000%! But on Wednesday, the shares (7) _____ as much as 21% at one point before (8) _____ in the last hour of trading to end the day up 11%.

Unit 8 Explaining Financial Data 81

Speaking

8 Work in pairs to describe this graph. One of you should talk about overheads and the other talks about profits.

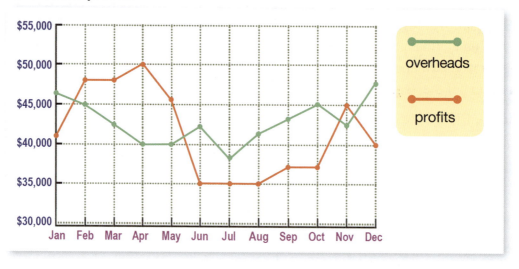

Writing

9 You are a broker and one of your clients has asked you to prepare a report on the performance of his investment portfolio. Use the information and notes below to write your report (120–140 words).

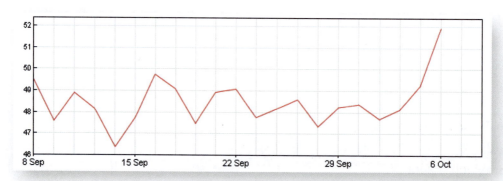

Useful language for reports

- This report looks at / deals with…
- The current situation is…
- The key events/figures show that…
- It can be seen that…
- As far as…is concerned…

- Firstly/Secondly/Finally
- Nevertheless/However / In spite of
- Furthermore / In addition / Moreover
- In conclusion / To sum up

positive effect on stock market

give reasons why

Market Events (8 Sep. to 6 Oct.)
- Black Tuesday hit NYSE first, then the other major markets
- Strong dollar at the end of September
- Slow growth predicted for rest of October

explain which stock market client's investments are in

Technical Terms

FTSE 100 index 　　金融时报100指数
FTSE 250 index 　　金融时报250指数
Black Tuesday 　　　黑色星期二

Unit 8 Explaining Financial Data

UNIT 9 Digital Payment

Learning Objectives

Upon completion of the unit, students will be able to:

- compare the similarities and differences between the two most popular digital payment methods in China;
- know the functions of digital payment;
- know the trends of digital payment in China.

Unit 9   Digital Payment

Starting Off

1 Read the text below and discuss with your partner. What's your favourite payment method during the pandemic? In addition to shopping, where else can you use it?

After the COVID-19 **epidemic** was known in China, the Payment & Clearing Association of China (PCAC) launched an action on February 28, 2020 to encourage people to use mobile payment, online payment, and QR payment to avoid the risk of **infection**. As a result, in April 2020, the number of digital payments for **virtual** mobile phone transactions on a daily basis increased by 48.5% year on year. In terms of Alipay, the payment **frequency** of **sightseeing spots** has increased by 120%. On the other hand, WeChat Pay use for restaurants has increased by 447% compared with March 2020.

MY GLOSSARY

epidemic	n.	传染病,流行病	frequency	n.	频率;频繁
infection	n.	感染,传染;影响	sightseeing spot		游览点,观光景点
virtual	adj.	虚拟的			

Reading 1

WeChat Pay & Alipay

The most popular Chinese companies for digital payments are WeChat Pay and Alipay.

The main difference between these two companies is that WeChat Pay is an in-app **feature** of the social media app WeChat (*wexin* in Chinese), but Alipay is a **dedicated** mobile payment system.

WeChat Pay is a digital wallet. In China, WeChat Pay customers can make in-store payments for goods and services, top up a mobile phone account, pay for **utilities**, and order goods and services from virtual stores and bricks-and-mortar locations for delivery via WeChat mini-apps. WeChat then lets customers track those deliveries, request **refunds**, and easily reorder from the order history. In WeChat, a customer can **scan** a **bar code** in-store to check if the item is cheaper online.

With Alipay's mobile payment system app, Chinese customers can make the same in-store payments for goods and services, as well as order goods and services from Taobao and Tmall, as both are brands within the Alibaba Group, who also owns Alipay. WeChat Pay is not a digital payment option for either Taobao or Tmall.

MY GLOSSARY

feature	n.	特征, 特色
dedicated	adj.	专用的, 专门的
utility	n.	公用事业

refund	n.	退款; 退税
scan	v.	扫描; 浏览
bar code		条形码

2 Read the text and decide if the sentences below are true (*T*) or false (*F*). If there is not enough information, choose "doesn't say" (*DS*).

		T	F	DS
1)	WeChat Pay has a higher market penetration rate compared with Alipay.	☐	☐	☐
2)	Both WeChat Pay and Alipay can top up a mobile phone account and pay for utilities.	☐	☐	☐
3)	There are two ways to pay via QR code with WeChat Pay.	☐	☐	☐
4)	WeChat Pay is a digital payment option for Taobao.	☐	☐	☐
5)	WeChat Pay and Alipay have the same user fees.	☐	☐	☐

Unit 9   Digital Payment

Speaking 1

3 Look at the graph below about China's most popular digital services. Discuss with your partner about how often the surveyed respondents use digital financial services and for what.

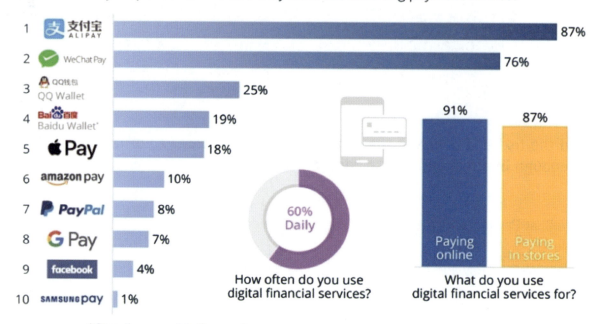

Listening

4 Listen to the conversation and answer the questions below.

1) What are they talking about?

2) What digital payment methods do they mention?

5 Listen to the recording and fill in the blanks.

There is a feature of WeChat called (1) _____. I'll show you how to connect that to your new bank account at Bank of China. Once that is done, you only have to carry cash for emergencies like (2) _____ or (3) _____. You'll use this digital payment option for everything in person as well with mini-apps in WeChat plus regular apps and websites. I even use it to buy movies on my television here.

Well, actually there is another one called (4) _____ that is also popular and also lets you buy stuff from Taobao and Tmall. You'll want to find things for your apartment, clothes, and everything else from those two huge (5) _____. Especially when you have a lot to buy at once and don't know your way around Beijing, those two sites are the best for good deals, (6) _____ and convenience. You can also use (7) _____ almost everywhere you use WeChat Pay, but there aren't as many mini-apps with Alipay. Also, you will want WeChat Pay to be able to transfer money in groups and have fun with (8) "_____".

Unit 9 Digital Payment

Reading 2

The Function of Payment

One of the most common digital payment function for both WeChat Pay and Alipay is payment. There are two ways to pay via **QR codes**.

With the first, the customer scans the seller's QR code with his mobile phone, which is displayed virtually or printed on a sign at the checkout counter, on a vending machine, etc. Then, the customer types in the amount to pay, sending the money to the seller via the digital payment app.

With the other method, the seller enters the amount due into his mobile phone or a commercial **handheld** scanning device. Then, the customer shows his personal QR code on his mobile phone, and the seller scans the QR code with his phone or device. In comparison, in Western countries where Apple Pay is available, a seller must buy Apple's technology to receive a payment.

The Function of Transfer

Another common digital payment function for WeChat Pay and Alipay is transfer. For example, if a group eats out together, then one person pays the total bill. Afterwards, that person sends a bill request to a WeChat Group Chat and instantly collects the money from the other people through transfers. Alipay also offers online transfer for customers, but it is not as convenient as WeChat.

Also **exclusive** to WeChat Pay is the Chinese culturally popular "red envelope" (*hongbao* in Chinese), a gift of money, which is common with families and other close relationships, in particular during the Spring Festival (Chinese New Year). Traditionally, the gift of money is presented in a red envelope. As an **alternative**, WeChat Pay offers a virtual "red envelope" function. During the Spring Festival of 2019, around 823 million people sent or received a WeChat "red envelope" in China.

MY GLOSSARY

QR code	二维码	exclusive	*adj.* 独有的, 排外的, 专一的
handheld	*adj.* 掌上的, 手持式的	alternative	*n.* 二中择一; 供替代的选择

6 Read the text and answer the questions below.

1) What is the difference between Chinese digital payment methods and Apple Pay?

_____

2) Which digital payment is your favourite? Why?

_____

3) When will people use "red envelope"?

_____

Speaking 2

7 How often do you use the "red envelope" of WeChat in your daily life? Do you think virtual "red envelopes" are as warm-hearted and traditional as receiving paper money in real red envelopes? Why?

Reading 3

Trends of Digital Payment in China

According to statistics released in early 2020 by the People's Bank of China (PBOC), 62.1 billion electronic payments were processed in 2018, including 30.7 billion mobile digital payment transactions, representing a year-on-year increase of 73.6%. As of March 2020, just over 776 million people were using mobile digital payments in China.

A survey by Nielsen and Alipay, in 2018, showed that mobile digital payments in the Chinese **outbound** tourism market saw an increase in both the rate of use (69%, up 4% from 2017) and the **proportion** of transactions (32%, **overtaking** cash for the first time). 91% of Chinese tourists said they would shop more and 93% of them would increase their spending if overseas **merchants** had digital payments through Alipay and/or WeChat Pay.

MY GLOSSARY

outbound	adj.	驶向外国的, 向外去的	overtake	v.	赶上, 追上, 超过
proportion	n.	比例, 占比	merchant	n.	商人

Unit 9   Digital Payment   91

8 Read the text and decide if the sentences below are true (*T*) or false (*F*). If there is not enough information, choose "doesn't say" (*DS*).

	T	F	DS
1) More and more people use mobile digital payments in China.	☐	☐	☐
2) The foreigners prefer to use mobile digital payments through Alipay in China.	☐	☐	☐
3) Chinese tourists will shop more if overseas merchants can pay by Alipay or WeChat Pay.	☐	☐	☐

Speaking 3

9 Will it change your outbound tourism plans whether or not a foreign country offers Chinese digital payment options? Why? Discuss with your partner.

Writing

10 Write a short essay (120–150 words) explaining at least three advantages of Chinese digital payment options for a Chinese outbound tourist or a foreigner visiting or living in China.

92　银行与金融英语

Technical Terms

Payment & Clearing Association of China   中国支付清算协会
digital payment   数字支付
digital wallet   数字钱包
checkout counter   付款柜台, 收银台
vending machine   自动贩卖机, 自动售货机

UNIT 10 Applying for a Job

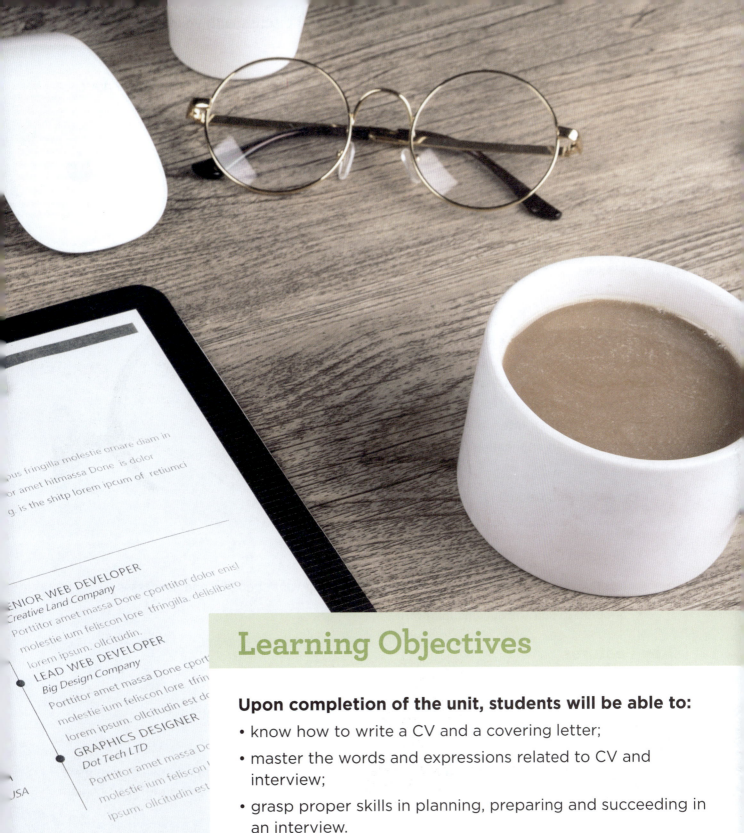

Learning Objectives

Upon completion of the unit, students will be able to:
- know how to write a CV and a covering letter;
- master the words and expressions related to CV and interview;
- grasp proper skills in planning, preparing and succeeding in an interview.

Starting Off

1 Tick the things you would expect to see in a CV and discuss with your partner.

- ☐ address
- ☐ interests
- ☐ qualifications
- ☐ career history
- ☐ marital status
- ☐ social media presence
- ☐ date of birth
- ☐ name
- ☐ favourite TV programmes
- ☐ nickname

Reading 1

How to Write a CV

A **curriculum vitae**, CV for short, is a brief **summary** of facts about you and your **qualifications**, work history, skills and experience. It is **essential** to have a good CV when **applying for** a job as it is your chance to sell yourself and be selected for an **interview**. Some companies may ask you to fill in an **application form** instead of sending a CV.

Your CV should be:

- printed on white paper and no more than 2 or 3 sides;
- clear and correct;
- positive and make a good impression, **emphasising** your strengths and successes;
- adapted to suit the specific job **profile**.

Key Features

Personal details
Your name, address, phone number(s), email address and date of birth.

Personal profile
This is normally at the beginning of the CV. It is a short statement aimed at selling yourself so you should use positive words and expressions. It must be **specifically** written for the position you are applying for.

Work experience
It is normal practice to list your most recent job first, with the dates. It is not a good idea to leave any **gaps** between dates and if you do not have a lot of experience, you should include details of part-time and **voluntary** work.

Qualifications and training
This includes qualifications from school and university as well as any other training courses or **certificates**. You should indicate the date (the most recent first), the title of the qualification, the level obtained and the organisation/place.

Achievements/Skills/Competences
This can include foreign languages and computer skills, as well as things like artistic or musical skills. It is possible to **highlight** a particular achievement—personal or **professional**—which **reflects** well on your ability to do the job.

Interests
Hobbies or sports activities can help show particular abilities or skills which could be relevant for the job.

References
This **section** is for the name, position and **contact details** of at least two people who can provide a personal and/or work reference. **Alternatively** it is possible to state that references can be supplied on request.

MY GLOSSARY

curriculum vitae		简历, 履历	voluntary	adj. 自愿的
summary	n.	总结, 小结	certificate	n. 证书, 证明
qualification	n.	资格, 资历	achievement	n. 成绩, 成就
essential	adj.	必要的, 至关重要的	competence	n. 能力, 才干
apply for		应聘, 申请	highlight	v. 强调; 突出
interview	n.	面试, 面谈	professional	adj. 专业的; 职业的
application form		申请表	reflect	v. 反映; 反射
emphasise	v.	强调	reference	n. 推荐信, 介绍信
profile	n.	简况, 简介	section	n. 部分
specifically	adv.	专门地; 明确地, 具体地	contact detail	联系方式
gap	n.	间隔期; 差距	alternatively	adv. 或者, 要不

2 Read the text and discuss the questions below.

1) What is the purpose of a CV?
2) How long should it be? Why do you think that is?

Unit 10 Applying for a Job

3) Is it a good idea to use the same CV for different job applications? Why / Why not?

4) Why do you think the personal profile is normally at the start of the CV?

5) What order should you list your qualifications and previous jobs? Why do you think that is?

6) What kind of interests do you think would be positive to include in your CV?

7) What is the purpose of indicating references?

8) Can you think of examples of positive words and expressions for a CV?

Speaking 1

3 Look at this example CV and say whether it follows all the advice given in Reading 1. Discuss with your partner.

Peter Bowland

Address 7 High Street, Rochford, SS4 7PT
Phone 01702 986631
Email peter.bowland@virgin.net

Personal profile
I am highly motivated and work well as part of a team. My overseas professional experience at The Silver Ivy—Hotel and Conference Centre, Gibraltar as Security Supervisor taught me to adapt to new situations and to work under challenging conditions and high standard levels. I am now looking for a position as a Security Manager to develop my career and duties.

Qualifications

2009–2012 Associates degree in Criminal Justice
Manchester University

2006–2008 Certification in Security Management
Hope Sixth Form College, Luton

Work history

November 2012 Security Supervisor at The Silver Ivy—Hotel and Conference Centre, Gibraltar

Sept. 2008–June 2009 Deputy Security Supervisor at Johnson's Hall Conference Centre, Leeds

Interests I enjoy scuba diving and water sports. I started sports as a team player with basketball.

References
Dr Craig Knowles
Hotel Manager at The Silver Ivy—Hotel and Conference Centre,

Ms Susan Knight
General Manager Johnson's Hall Conference Centre, Leeds

4 Read this job advertisement and discuss the questions below. Then discuss with your partner the suitability of the candidate in Exercise 3 for this job advertisement.

1) What position is being advertised?
2) What requisites are they looking for?
3) Does the candidate have the right experience? And qualifications?
4) Does the CV make a positive impression? Why / Why not?

5 Suppose you are the interviewee for this job, how would you introduce yourself in the first interview so that the interviewer will give you an opportunity to have the job?

6 Have you ever seen a Europass CV? How do you think it differs from a standard CV? Talk together.

The Europass CV is a standard document aimed at simplifying the job application process between EU member states for both employers and applicants. It is possible to complete the CV online or to download it, together with examples and instructions on how to fill it in.

There are five Europass documents designed to make your skills and qualifications clearly and easily understood in Europe. In addition to the CV, there is the European Skills Passport, which includes a Language Passport, Europass Mobility, Certificate Supplement and Diploma Supplement.

The European Skills passport can be attached to the Europass CV to give comprehensive details of your skills and qualifications, grouping together copies of certificates and degrees and proof of employment.

Europass also offers the possibility to compile covering letters and gives suggestions for key expressions for each part.

Europass Curriculum Vitae

Personal information

First name(s)/Surname(s)	**Sabina Cerratani**
Address	Via Monte Bianco 428, 20131 Milan (Italy)
Mobile	330 9000012345
Email(s)	sabi_cerra@gmail.com
Nationality	Italian
Date of birth	02/09/1995
Gender	Female

Desired employment/ Occupational field	**Publishing and translating**

Work experience

Dates	12/2014 →
Occupation or position held	Editorial Assistant
Main activities and responsibilities	Translation of correspondence into English and Spanish Assisting at international book fairs
Name and address of employer	GFR SpA Via Torino, 20123 Milan (Italy)
Type of business or sector	Publishing

Education and training

Dates	2010/2014
Title of qualification awarded	Italian High School Certificate
Name and type of organisation providing education and training	IISS Pietro Vieri (Business High School) Via Lattanzio, Milano (Italy)

Personal skills and competences

Mother tongue(s)	**Italian**
Other language(s)	

Self-assessment	Understanding				Speaking				Writing	
European level (*)	Listening		Reading		Spoken interaction		Spoken production			
English	C1	Proficient user	C1	Proficient user	C1	Proficient user	C1	Proficient user	C1	Proficient user
Spanish	B2	Independent user	B2	Independent user	C1	Proficient user	C1	Proficient user	B2	Independent user

(*) Common European Framework of Reference (CEF) level

Social skills and competences	Ability to adapt to multicultural environments, thanks to extensive travel
Organisational skills and competences	Excellent coordination skills developed during 2 years as Editor of school newspaper
Computer skills and competences	Microsoft Office
Artistic skills and competences	Sculpture
Other skills and competences	Interested in travel, world food, cinema
Driving licence(s)	B
Additional information	Reference: Mr P. Sagripanti, Principal, IIIS Pietro Verri, Milan

Reading 2

How to Write a Covering Letter

Jeremy Keystone
7 High Street
Rochford
SS4 7PT
Tel: 01702 986631
jeremy.keystone@virgin.net

Ms Lewis Carol,
Celtic Security Ltd.,
83 Wimbledon Park Side, London
SW19 5LP

17th April 20..

Dear Ms Lewis,

> Here you should refer to the advertisement and where you saw it. Include the **title** of the position and any reference number.

I am writing in response to your **advertisement** in *The Guardian* and wish to apply for the **post** of Director of Security.

> Here you can give a few details about your qualifications and/or experience.

After training school, where I gained knowledge and related skills in carrying out security operations and procedures in accordance to prescribed rules and regulations, I started working as Deputy Security Supervisor, then I attended Manchester University to deepen my knowledge in Security. Since graduation I have been working as Security Supervisor at a five star superior hotel. My strengths can be summed up as follows:

- Extensive experience in handling general security operations including facility inspection, updating of paper work and security manuals
- Demonstrated ability to command and control FCC activities during emergency situations
- Well versed in reviewing and investigating accidental and misconduct reports and issuing future course of action in light of incident analysis
- Able to assess staff and personnel training needs and provide training accordingly

> This is your chance to state why you would be perfect for the company. Do not just use the same letter for every job application. Each letter should be **tailored** to the specific **requisites** mentioned in the ad.

Having worked for two international security groups, my skills in security management have been refined by experience. With a 10+ years' career in the security field, I feel confident that I can contribute significantly to the role of Director of Security at Smithson's Medical Group.

> Here you can mention any **enclosures** (CV, references, certificates) and state how you are going to follow up on your letter.

Please find **enclosed** my Curriculum Vitae and I would welcome the opportunity to provide further information during an interview.

I look forward to hearing from you.

Yours sincerely,

Jeremy Keystone

Jeremy Keystone
Enc.

Unit 10   Applying for a Job

MY GLOSSARY

advertisement   n. 广告，宣传
post   n. 职位，要职
title   n. 职位名称；职称
tailor   v. 专门制作；使适应特定需要
requisite   n. 必要条件；必需品
enclose   v. 随函附上
enclosure   n. （信中）附件

7 Read the text and answer the questions below.

1) Why is a covering letter important?

2) How should a covering letter be written?

3) How does a covering letter usually start?

4) Should a covering letter repeat all the details of a CV? Why / Why not?

5) Why is it not a good idea to use a standard covering letter for all applications?

Writing

8 Sabina Cerratani wants to apply for this job. Use the details of her CV in Exercise 6 and write her covering letter. Also include these points:

- you saw the advertisement in *The Telegraph*;
- you will be in London in two weeks so would be available for an interview;
- you have travelled a lot in South America because your mother is from Argentina.

Little Bear Publishing House PLC
7 West Lane, London W1

SENIOR EDITORAL ASSISTANT
£22,800 – £26,200

We are a well-known publisher specializing in children's fiction, translated into over 17 languages. The position of Senior Editorial Assistant is based in London, but the candidate must be willing to travel, especially in Europe and South America. Good knowledge of Microsoft Office and minimum five years' experience in a similar field are essential.
Apply to Mr Clune, quoting ref SEA 25.

Reading 3

Tips for a Successful Interview

Job interviews can be stressful; however, with the proper planning and preparation, you can get the job. Read these tips to help you survive the interview and get the **job offer**.

Before the Interview
- Research the company and prepare relevant questions. **Interviewers** appreciate when job **candidates** show interest in the company and **available** position.

- Organise all **paperwork**, including your CV and **eventual** references from previous employers.

- Plan **responses** to common interview questions and practise interviewing with a **peer**.

- Prepare for questions about **salary** expectations by finding out how much employees in the position you are applying for are **typically** paid.

During the Interview
- Make a good first impression by arriving on time for the interview. Make sure to dress in clean and professional **attire**. Finally, be polite and use the interviewer's name when speaking.

- **Respond** to all questions clearly. Interviewees should provide **solid** examples of how their previous experience relates to skills needed for the new position. Also be sure to explain your future career goals.

After the Interview
- Employers may request a **call-back** to obtain more information as a **follow-up**.

MY GLOSSARY

job offer		工作机会
interviewer	n.	面试考官, 主持面试者
candidate	n.	候选人, 申请人
available	adj.	可获得的; 可用的
paperwork	n.	文件; 文书工作
eventual	adj.	最终的; 有条件的
response	n.	响应, 反应, 回答
peer	n.	同龄人, 同辈
salary	n.	工资, 薪水
typically	adv.	通常, 一般
attire	n.	（尤指特定样式或正式的）服装, 衣着
respond	v.	回答, 回应
solid	adj.	可靠的, 可信赖的
call-back	n.	回电
follow-up	n.	后续（行动）

9 Read the text and decide if these sentences are true (*T*) or false (*F*). Then correct the false ones.

T　F

1) A job candidate should ask about the company during the interview. ☐ ☐

2) Interviewees make a good impression by dressing professionally for the interview. ☐ ☐

3) A call-back is a typical way for a job candidate to follow up after an interview. ☐ ☐

4) Talking about career goals and salary is not recommended. ☐ ☐

5) Prepare your CV and references before the interview. ☐ ☐

6) Before the interview find out about the company via the Web. ☐ ☐

Speaking 2

10 Which of the points in Reading 3 do you think are the most important? Why? Can you think of any other Dos and Don'ts for an interview?

11 How long do you think it takes an interviewer to have a basic impression of a candidate? What do you think a candidate can do to make sure his/her first impression is positive?